Is there a
DRY DRUNK
in your life?

By
Carole Bennett, M.A.

SEA·HILL
PRESS

In order to maintain the anonymity of people mentioned in this book, their names as well as some identifying characteristics and details such as physical properties, occupations, and places of residence have been changed.

In an effort to avoid gender bias and gender gimmicks as well as awkward writing, the author/editor(s) have implemented the use of the singular *they* and its inflected or derivative forms to refer to a single person.

Ordering Information: Special rates are available on quantity purchases by corporations, associations, and others. For details, please direct inquiries to orders@seahillpress.com.

Sea Hill Press Inc.
P. O. Box 60301
Santa Barbara, California 93160
www.seahillpress.com

ISBN: 978-1-937720-31-5

Printed in the United States of America

Is there a
DRY DRUNK
in your life?

AND OTHER UNSETTLING

QUESTIONS ... AND ANSWERS

By
Carole Bennett, M.A.

Disclaimers

This book contains information that is intended to help the readers be better informed about substance abuse issues and to provide information and motivation to our readers. The statements, opinions and data contained in this publication are solely the expression and opinion of its individual author. No warranties or guarantees are expressed or implied by the publisher's choice to include any of the content in this volume. The publisher and the editor(s) disclaim responsibility for any injury to persons or property resulting from any ideas, methods, instructions or products referred to in the content of this book. It is sold with the understanding that the publisher is not engaged to render any type of psychological, legal, or any other kind of professional advice.

The methods describe within this book are the author's personal thoughts. They are not intended to be a definitive set of instructions for resolving family issues. The information contained is not intended as a substitute for the medical advice of a licensed physician. Should a serious family condition develop or exist, seek professional assistance from your doctor or family therapist. If you feel personally threatened within your situation, immediately call local authorities or the police for immediate assistance.

This information contained in this book is not intended as legal advice, for legal advice has to be tailored to the specific circumstances and facts of each situation. Consult an attorney before taking any action based on information contained in this book. Neither the publisher, editors, nor author shall be liable for any physical, psychological, emotional, financial, or commercial damages, including, but not limited to, special, incidental, consequential or other damages. Our views and rights are the same: You are responsible for your own choices, actions, and results.

CONTENTS

INTRODUCTION   1

CHAPTER 1 – What is a "dry drunk"?   5

CHAPTER 2 – What do addiction and relapse really look like?   13

CHAPTER 3 – When is it time to throw in the towel?   37

CHAPTER 4 – Is it important to seek outside help?   51

CHAPTER 5 – Why is the alcoholic/addict so self-destructive?   59

CHAPTER 6 – Why are the recovery contract, boundaries, and expectations important?   65

CHAPTER 7 – Why is being an enabler to the alcoholic/addict so dangerous and detrimental?   93

CHAPTER 8 – Why is it difficult to communicate with the alcoholic/addict?   105

CHAPTER 9 – Are others judgmental of the loved ones of alcoholic/addicts?   117

CHAPTER 10 – How does one rebuild trust with the alcoholic/addict?   123

CHAPTER 11 – What is it like to deal with a loved one who is an alcoholic/addict?   127

CHAPTER 12 – Is it possible to move on toward a healthier tomorrow?   147

CHAPTER 13 – What other advice can you offer to help a loved one dealing with an alcoholic/addict?   163

INTRODUCTION

When my publisher suggested that I start thinking about writing another book, I felt that I had already covered all the pertinent and important topics in my previous book, *Reclaim Your Life: You and the Alcoholic/Addict.* However, I started contemplating how I could hone in on some of the most common questions, concerns, and issues that keep coming up from my clients and readers.

It seems to me that the same confusing, unsettling, disheartening, and well, I could go on and on, topics continue to surface regarding the devastating, infuriating, and sometimes totally bizarre behavior from the alcoholic/addicts in our lives. Since areas like communication, boundaries, expectations, goals, relapse, and enabling appear to be the focal point of many discussions, I thought I would target this book to those issues and process some answers.

Unlike my first book, which touches on some of these concerns, this book will go more in-depth, looking at some of the most perplexing and baffling areas we as parents, spouses, siblings, family, and friends deal with when we love an alcoholic/addict. In addition, I have shared some personal experiences with alcoholics/addicts in my own life. My ex-husband and daughter have been the mainstay of many of my columns. Through each sad, painful, frustrating, fearful experience, I have learned something more about their addictions as well as helped myself in my own recovery.

One thing I have come to appreciate in all these many years of working with families besieged with their loved ones' addiction issues is that concepts need to be repeated over and over. Sometimes peering through a different angle or viewpoint and asking diverse questions may prompt a new look for the family to examine. In turn, this will help in navigating those murky waters of addiction and recovery. The world of addiction, recovery, and relapse is like being lost in one of those old-fashioned house-of-mirrors exhibits, where there doesn't seem to be any way out. But be patient, because in time you can face some unpleasant but honest reality issues and come to understand what your role is in this scenario. You will come to understand that no one possesses any special powers to cure the alcoholic/addict of their life of addiction.

No one wants to think that the mate chosen for life or a wonderful son or special daughter has a habit that has taken over their life. Your heart breaks in two pieces: one half feels the pain and suffering your loved one is going through, and the other half can't help but question what you did wrong and how you can fix it. When you love another person, you do feel awful if they are in pain and you can't help. And for that, you have a green light for a broken heart. But the self-questioning half is more about ego, shame, and embarrassment because you think it puts into question your ability as a family member or friend. Please, please try to abolish that concept.

Every human being captains their own ship, can and does make decisions on their own, and picks their own path to follow. No matter how many safety nets we put along the way, the alcoholic/addict will avoid them, cut through them, and do whatever it takes to sail their life into a destructive storm. The sooner you come to grips with that, the better off you will be for exploring and forging your own very important recovery.

At the end of each chapter I have included a processing questionnaire that will help you create a blueprint to focus on your own course of action. Be honest when answering these questions. Write out your answers, then revisit the questionnaires weekly, monthly, or whenever you feel you need to. Are you accomplishing your objectives? Or do you need a shot in the arm to get you back on track? No one is going to read your answers unless you offer them, so let your hair down and write out all those thoughts that maybe you have kept in the basement for a long time. Consider what you write to be your recovery plan to gauge and monitor your own progress with your qualifier, the alcoholic/addict. My hope is that such an exercise will in a sense empower you to be accountable to your personal goals and expectations.

Write down issues surrounding not only the alcoholic/addict in your life but also life outside of addiction, life for your own living. So often we lose ourselves in the continued uphill struggle with the alcoholic/addicts in our lives. So let's start right here with the first processing question.

Processing Questionnaire

- What do you hope to get out of this book?

CHAPTER 1

WHAT IS A "DRY DRUNK"?

As habitual as migrating birds, clients have come to me thrilled that their loved one has stopped drinking, yet they report that the partnership is as brittle as tinder and inexplicably worse than before. Confusion abounds as both have desired sobriety, yet now that it is here, they wonder why the relationship seems to be on rockier ground than when the alcoholic was drinking. This can be the world of the "dry drunk," whether referring to an alcoholic or a drug addict; however, here I refer only to the alcoholic.

What is a "dry drunk"? In putting the pieces together from my personal experiences as well as my clients' stories, the description seems to be universal: one who abstains from alcohol but is still grappling with the emotional and psychological maladies that may have fueled their addiction to begin with and that continue to have a stranglehold on their psyche. Remember that alcohol and addiction was the fiber and a substantial, if not total, embodiment of their being.

If any of us were to stop participating in something that we were used to doing for years, something that was a substantial part of our daily existence, then in conjunction with the physical aspect we also would need additional help emotionally and psychologically in working through the absence.

The alcoholic needs and should want to be responsible for all aspects of their recovery, whether it is through a 12-step program or a professional substance abuse counselor. Without these forms of support, their growth in recovery could be stunted with having only one piece of the pie, that of being physically clean and sober.

The alcoholic needs to realize that this part of recovery needs as much work as the physical addiction does. Without working on the emotional/psychological portion, the alcoholic may become lazy, irritable, easily annoyed, or quick to anger and will defend and justify at the slightest questioning or provocation.

I have listed nine dispositions of the "dry drunk" that can hit the recovering alcoholic hard in the honest light of sobriety in addition to putting added strain and pressure on relationships. Your loved one may not know how to handle these realizations, and consequently they may use you as a punching bag for their frustration and discontent.

9 dispositions of the dry drunk:

1. Resentful toward a family member or friend who has made them "stop drinking or else . . . "

2. Annoyed and frustrated with the realization that they can't drink like a "normie" ever again.

3. Disappointed that because of their drinking they may have not realized goals, dreams, and potentials and are wondering if it's too late to achieve, or if they are even capable of achieving, those goals or dreams.

4. Uncomfortable with having to accept and take responsibility for the years wasted due to drinking, without looking for an excuse or justification.

5. Anxious about venturing out or challenging themselves for fear of failure. The alcoholic may not have had any normal life experience with failure and success, which would have made them stronger and wiser. Instead those years were void of dealing with life on life's terms due to their addiction.

6. Jealous of others for their stick-to-it-tiveness, perseverance, and strength. Envious of the family member or friend for their dreams, punishing them by not being supportive, questioning their ability, and striving to clip their wings of creativity.

7. Depressed at having to give up or losing their go-to buddy of booze in times of happiness or stress.

8. Distressed by a mind still pecking away at them that needs and wants a drink. Though physically not drinking, they have been in this pattern for many years.

9. Crabby and angry while dealing with emotions that are very close to the surface. Anger and a short fuse are all too common.

8 states of mind we might experience while having a dry drunk prominent in our lives:

1. A "walking on eggshells" feeling every time we are around them.

2. Wondering which person will come through the door. Will it be the nice or nasty person?

3. Anxious about making plans since we don't want to expose anyone else to a hair-trigger outburst of anger or discontent.

4. Frustrated and exhausted about trying to stay one step ahead of what might provoke an unpleasant incident.

5. Questioning continuity and trust. Making plans is sketchy at best, all depending on the state of mind of the dry drunk.

6. Acquiescing more because either we feel guilty or we feel we are the reason our loved one stopped their addiction in the first place. We need to make everything extra nice so they know how much we appreciate what they have given up.

7. Buying into the theory that them giving up their addiction is enough, so they don't have to work on any other aspects of their life in order to achieve a full and healthy recovery.

8. Feeling we should be grateful that they have stopped drinking

and, therefore, should not demand anything else from them as that would make us appear to be lacking empathy or not to be supportive enough.

Phew! . . . that's a lot of garbage to trudge through. It's not uncommon for many to say that it was easier to deal with the alcoholic in their life when they were drinking. But that's a sad and unfortunate way to look at things. After all, who wants to hold their breath (actually or figuratively), be on pins and needles, or walk on eggshells on a daily basis? It doesn't leave much room for fun or relaxing.

An open mind and positive attitude is a good place for the recovering alcoholic to start, and it is imperative for them to deal with the painful issues that might have brought them to their addiction in the first place. This is the only way for any real progress toward a clean and healthy lifestyle to take form.

Though this may sound sophomoric, the alcoholic needs to pursue another passion other than their drug of choice, whether it's collecting stamps, returning to school, or rebuilding an old Mustang. They need to pursue anything that will break old habits and deter them from resentments and a woe-is-me attitude and will help them instead to strive toward healthy alternatives. Feeling good about personal accomplishments and self-respecting goals is strong emotional medicine for the alcoholic working on their recovery.

If these objectives can become standard operating procedure, the alcoholic can and will come to appreciate the need for expanding their clean and sober lifestyle beyond the act of just not indulging in their addiction. It stands to reason that if your loved one can funnel energy toward healthy productive objectives, they will be successful in leaving the negative disposition of "dry drunk" by the wayside.

I have had many clients and friends alike tell me that they are in a relationship with someone who has all the personality traits of a dry drunk but who doesn't drink or only drinks socially. They ask if there is a difference—or is being an asshole fairly universal, regardless of what propels them to that place?

Some people are just plain moody. Their day depends on whether they wake up on the right side of the bed or not. I know for myself, I couldn't live with a moody person as I would have a tough time wondering who was coming through the door at night and hoping that it had been a good day so Mr. Moody would be in a good mood. Also, I don't want to have to follow the bouncing ball all evening or throughout the weekend wondering if the slightest situation may turn a good mood into a sour mood.

Processing Questionnaire

The first few questions are easy, whereas the later ones are the toughies. Be honest with your answers. You are the only one reading this, and no one is looking over your shoulder judging your answers or progress.

I strongly suggest that you give yourself simple, doable goals to accomplish. In a few weeks, look back at what you wrote and evaluate yourself on your progress. Make whatever adjustments you may need to in order to have more success the next time around.

- Who is the dry drunk in your life?

  My husband

- What are some of the characteristics that this person possesses that puts them into this category?

  moody
  angry
  walk on eggshells

- What has been done (if anything) to date to bring these distasteful characteristics to this person's attention?

  anger
  resentment
  therapy

- If you have voiced your opinion, what was the outcome?

  he gets angry
  confrontation

- Did you feel the outcome was successful? If so, for how long?

  no

- If unsuccessful, what is your plan to change things? ("I will not be around when I know that the dry drunk is at their worse. I will do volunteer work during those times or do something that gets me out of their way.")

- How do you see this happening? ("I will politely and quietly leave the room if I'm feeling uncomfortable or badgered. I'll take a walk around the block the first time, go to a movie the second time, stay overnight at a friend's house the third time.")

- What is my time frame for change to occur? ("Every month or six weeks I will regroup with myself and see if things have changed or if I need to augment things.")

- What are the consequences/boundaries that you will enforce if nothing changes? (If you have already implemented the examples in number 6, it may be time to take more serious action. That doesn't mean filing for divorce or writing your child out of the will. It may mean asking your child to live elsewhere if they continue to sport their addiction and be rude and indignant. It may mean asking for your spouse to move out for awhile as you are not wishing to continue being their personal punching bag.)

- What are your personal thoughts? (Where is your head at today? How can you take small steps to take care of yourself?)

CHAPTER 2

WHAT DO ADDICTION AND RELAPSE REALLY LOOK LIKE?

There are probably more roads that can lead to addiction than there are microchips in a computer. With each year of counseling, lecturing, and writing, I am always fascinated by the creative and imaginative reasons one gives themselves as bona fide reasons for their out-of-line behavior. They give themselves a get-out-of-jail card because this or that happened to them when they were younger that has left a bottomless pit with them forever, a pit they can't seem to or don't want to climb out of.

I have had many clients come to me feeling almost angry with themselves for being so hard on the alcoholic/addict in their life because they finally heard from that loved one that they were molested by the babysitter, came from a broken home, were unpopular in school, couldn't compete scholastically or athletically, felt like an outsider, or were a bedwetter until close to puberty . . . and on and on.

Having been an innocent participant of unhappy circumstances bestowed upon them in their youth becomes their get-out-of-jail card for irresponsible and reckless behavior, as though it were their only way of dealing with such tragedy. Please understand that I am not belittling the unhappy, difficult experiences children have had while growing up, but the responsibility rests with that child-turned-adult to get help for the skeletons in the closet that make it difficult to deal with life on life's terms.

Addictions can come from psychological situations like I have touched on above. An addicted person may never touch an alcoholic beverage or drug substance in their life, but they still might have an addiction issue: anger displacement, eating disorder, health obsession, gambling addiction, sexual issue, etc. These addictions might not get them a DUI, but they can be just as destructive toward family and friends as alcohol or chemical addictions.

First, let's look at the physical, behavioral, and drug-specific symptoms, then we'll turn our attention to the most common roads to addiction as well as the common signs of relapse and common triggers toward relapse.

The first thing any family member or friend wants to be aware of is a significant change in a loved one's personality, physical appearance, attitude, or behavior. There's no need to hit the panic button right away, as it may just be a bad mood—not making the team at school, rejected by a friend, bad day at the office, or whatever—but if the state continues, then something else might be amiss.

12 physical signs of addiction:

1. Appetite: changes in eating habits and a loss or gain of weight

2. Physical condition: poor health; unsteadiness or wavering walk

3. Sleep habits: awake at unusual times; sleeping too much or not enough

4. Eyes: watery, red, or puffy eyes; pupils not normal; eyes express a blank stare

5. Hands: cold, sweaty, or shaking hands

6. Facial features: puffy, swollen, pale, or rosy complexion

7. Odor: alcohol or substance smell on clothes, body, or breath

8. Hyperactivity: amped up, very chatty, restless

9. Cold or flu-like symptoms: coughing, runny nose, nausea, vomiting, chills, sweating

10. Needle marks: dark veins, hard veins, lumps, and/or small spots on arms, legs, feet, neck, fingernails, etc.

11. Tremors: rhythmic shaking in hands, head, or feet

12. Heartbeat: irregular or rapid heart rate; high blood pressure

11 behavioral signs of addiction:

1. Changes in personality: overall change in attitude or character; loss of interest in family and family activities; changes in personal grooming habits: unkempt, dirty, tattoos

2. Changes in social life: new friends, new hangouts, new activities; loss of interest in doing what was once pleasurable and fun

3. Lack of interest: late for class or work, or not going at all; drop in grades or poor work performance; not completing tasks

4. Attention difficulties: inattentive, unfocused, forgetful, irresponsible

5. Changes in motivation: laziness; little or no motivation, energy, or self-esteem

6. Increased sensitivity: resentful and overly sensitive to criticism, or silly and giddy

7. Emotional changes: easily angered, moody, nervous, or paranoid

8. Greater secrecy: unreachable, uncommunicative, and suspicious behavior; frequent and long trips to the bathroom; frequently leaving on trips to the store, for long walks, or to meet someone

9. Legal issues: troubles with the law, car accidents, legal infractions

10. Need for money: stealing, selling, and pawning items

11. Possession: drugs, drug paraphernalia, interest in drug culture (posters, music, clothing, etc.)

5 drug-specific symptoms:

1. Alcohol: clumsiness, slurred speech; difficulty walking, driving, or doing everyday activities

2. Depressants: same symptoms as alcohol, but without the smell of alcohol

3. Stimulants: hyperactivity, euphoria, irritability, anxiety, excessive talking; followed by depression, sleeping, eating disorders

4. Hallucinogens: bizarre and irrational behavior, paranoia, aggression, hallucinations, mood swings, detachment, self-absorption, confusion

5. Heroin: needle marks, loss of appetite, sweating, vomiting, twitching, contracted pupils, no response to light

Now let's turn our attention to the emotional aspects of addiction. It goes without saying that if the family or neighborhood are involved with drugs and street crimes that the residents are more apt to participate in such than not. I am a big believer that an addiction gene can be passed down from generation to generation. If looks, disposition, and talent can be passed down, then why can't a gene for a propensity for addiction?

That having been said, the list of emotional aspects of addiction comes from the emotional or psyche state of the individual rather than circumstances that are out of their control.

Emotional aspects of addiction:

1. **Boredom**

As the saying goes, "An idle mind is the devil's playground." Anyone with too much time on their hands may find themselves in unsettling, troubled waters. People who easily feel bored tend to be weary or restless because of lack of any personal interests. They are difficult to motivate and oftentimes they feel lazy and find little joy in expanding their horizons or interests. They can often talk a good game like wanting to join a gym, buy a bicycle, work as a volunteer, or do something that will get them out of their rut. But truth to tell, they are *comfortable* in their rut and really don't want to put too much effort into changing.

They are bored with themselves, their jobs, and their life. Boredom usually stems from one's own lack of motivation, endeavor, or creativity. Everyone gets bored now and then, but the difference lies in changing that mood to a healthy alternative. It's easy to be bored with others of like mind, and if their entertainment comes from sitting around passing the pipe for a few high-flying hits, then they justify that they are socializing. Therefore, they are not bored anymore. Yawn. This kind of boredom can ultimately lead to an anti-social, destructive path toward addiction.

It's hard to imagine anyone being bored today; even if they are not interested in stretching their muscles, feelings, or minds. Computers, smartphones, media players, tablets, and game consoles can provide hours of activity (in my opinion, useless, nonproductive activity that if done solo makes for noninteraction with others, to boot). So it seems that one has to look hard and actually seek out being bored. If one is used to being bored, it will take some real perseverance to shake off. It is a state of mind and requires a committed determination to do something about it to change up the routine.

As I said previously, they can form a habit out of being bored because boredom can present a degree of comfort and safety. Eventually, since no one expects anything from them and, in turn, they don't expect anything from themselves, drugs and/or alcohol can seem like an acceptable choice of behavior. Using the easiest and quickest fix, requiring little or no effort, can take them to a place where they don't think they are bored anymore.

As difficult a challenge as boredom can be to overcome for anyone of any age, the answer lies in confronting and moving through and beyond the *causes* of boredom. Anyone experiencing significant levels of boredom needs to ask themselves what challenging and likely unpleasant experience they are attempting to avoid. Fear of trying something new or venturing out beyond one's comfort zone can psych someone into just vegging out; therefore, boredom becomes their friend and an illuminated sign pointing them toward a great escape to drugs/alcohol.

When children or adolescents are spending too much time in front of the television, or screens of any kind, or listlessly whiling away hours, it is time to step in. Curtail the screen-time hours and help your child look for and plan stimulating activities or hobbies. If they are not interested in pursuing them independently, then get involved yourself or recruit other members of the family. Strong, positive energy coupled with the right attitude is important to infuse into your child to shake the lazy, boring life and get with a new productive program. If executed early and properly, then boredom will have no opportunity to lead to dangerous experimentation with potentially addictive behaviors.

Adults who are active yet bored with work or mundane, tedious activities will have to push themselves to discover new adventures and make new friends. When a person has a job that represents a form of security but is painstakingly boring, they need to explore new possibilities for employment. Talking to family members and telling them of the boredom will provide support. Others can work with them in determining other paths to avoiding boredom. This might help to deter them from turning to alcohol or substance abuse in order to alleviate their boredom in a self-destructive, detrimental way. It also makes them accountable to those who have put out their hands to help.

Boredom is no fun. It's a waste of precious time and has zero productivity chips. Bored people need to become creative and shake things up in their lives. One never knows what might happen, especially when keeping an open mind. The alternatives are a stale, lackluster lifestyle or a life in which the only entertainment is destructive, out-of-control behavior. The aim is to take responsibility and choose the more creative and productive path.

2. **The desire to belong, be accepted, be popular**

Every person I've ever met—adult, teen, or child—wants some or all of the following: to belong, to be accepted, and to be popular with their peers. These desires are core emotional traits, and when void from our being, we feel unsettled and uncomfortable, regardless of our age.

No man (or woman) is an island. Close relationships, familiarity, and camaraderie represent the very definition of that warm and fuzzy feeling of belonging. Being accepted is a kissing cousin to belonging, for if one belongs, it stands to reason that one is accepted. Conversely, it would be difficult to belong if you were not accepted as well.

Let's start with the child or teenager who spends the bulk of their waking hours at school. Though it may not be cool to admit, they desperately desire to be a part of a clique or group. If they are able to find a healthy, productive niche, they will belong, be accepted, and be popular within that special community. This experience is not only good for the soul but also builds self-confidence and becomes a vital part of the formative years. Participating in this community instills a sense of commitment and accountability, not only to themselves but also to others. As adulthood approaches, this helps set the stage for building a self-assured career as well as for acting as part of a team in a work environment.

Looking back on our own childhoods, we can remember the various groups that everyone belonged to. There were the brainy or debate-team students, the nerdy and scientific sets, or the lofty sports figures and cheerleaders, among others. So what happens when our children or teenagers can't find that group that will give them a sense of belonging, acceptance, or popularity? Or when our child has found that group they so desperately want to be a part of but that wants no part of them?

As parents our hearts break as we witness our children or teenagers start to feel "less than," become self-critical, and possibly turn into their own worst enemies. Desperation might lead these children or teenagers into doing something they know is wrong and possibly dangerous.

Whether it is to score drugs, acquire alcohol, or even dabble in petty to serious criminal activity, these confused and scared children start to turn a deaf ear to morals, honesty, and values and begin to get caught up in a fast-moving current of destruction in order to fit in, be accepted, and supposedly be popular. If these characteristics start to sprout and consequently are not addressed, it is possible that the road to addiction could start here.

If you see or sense that your child or teenager has become lost or without direction, step in! If you are concerned about the company they are keeping just so they can be accepted or belong, step in!

Today, there is a wide range of positive, creative options offered to help your child or teenager find their own niche of acceptance and belonging. Some children and teens may need to be coaxed out of the negative signals and their narrow focus on what they have perceived as failure and rejection. Help them see different options while empathizing with how they feel.

As a parent, family member, or friend, you can help them explore what those different choices might be and tap into them in a positive and active way. Find a camp, after-school activity, club, group, or one-on-one tutor to help your child know and feel that they can be accepted and belong within their own group of interest. Work together to find what's comfortable for them (not you!).

This, of course, is all predicated upon an already established history of open, honest communication with your child; one in which they are accepted and have a strong sense of belonging in the family unit. If this is not the case, it would be unwise to pop up at the eleventh hour and try to redirect them. Your credibility may be questioned and these efforts could backfire, sending your child in the opposite direction and resulting in unhealthy, destructive behavior.

If eventually you believe that all honest and well-meaning endeavors have failed, then your options may take on a different approach. Though always reminding your child that you are there to turn to or talk to, you just may have to trust and hope that the child will come to their senses and abandon their destructive path. You can seek professional guidance and entertain other options such as a strict boarding school, out-patient program, or even an intervention. Keep in mind that each situation and scenario is different. It is the wise and thoughtful parent who weighs and considers every possibility very carefully for the health and welfare of their child.

3. **Low self-esteem**

Low self-esteem describes a substandard evaluation or disappointing appraisal of one's self-worth. Development of our self-esteem begins at the early stages of childhood and remains a part of our lives forever, shaping us toward one direction or another. The parent or guardian who is the focal point for raising the youngster has the power to either instill a sense of strong self-worth or one that is questionable or negative. In these early stages, everyone and everything can make an indelible impression.

We would like to believe that parents, guardians, and teachers are circles of support for our children, yet many of us came from households that said, "You are so stupid. Why can't you do anything right?"; or "You'll never amount to anything"; or "Why aren't you more like your brother/sister? Look how well he/she is doing!" These comments are thoughtless and cruel and produce so much negative energy that it could take substantially longer to undo the damage than it took to first sling those arrows. Such descriptive words forge indelible images. If they are not counteracted with loving, caring, and thoughtful communication, they could create a foundation of uncertainty, insecurity, and confusion—the perfect, fertile breeding ground for substance abuse.

If low self-esteem has been part of a teenager's upbringing, they may see themselves as less than everyone else, as deficient in one way or another. They may consider their body or looks to be undesirable; they may doubt their ability to participate in sports; or they may tell themselves that their brainpower is insufficient. In either child or adult, low self-esteem can result in feeling stuck and having little or no motivation or energy. Everything becomes drudgery. The attraction of escaping to a world where judgment is nonexistent becomes a very powerful hook.

Lack of self-esteem brings the potential for destructive behavior. It takes no special ability to participate in alcohol or illegal substance consumption. They think: Why not go for it? What is left to lose? The easy, effortless way is to take this lack of self-worth and drink it away into blackout or smoke it, snort it, or shoot it into oblivion.

I believe some alcoholics are shy, introverted people. Chances are they suffer from low self-esteem issues and have relied on the effects of alcohol to help them come out of their shells, be more gregarious, and approachable. The drinker may say, "Yeah, I need a few drinks in me to loosen me up." One has to be mindful that a few can easily turn into ten or twenty.

Lack of confidence is different from low self-esteem. For example; I have little or no confidence in my ability to be proficient on the computer, run a marathon, or paint a landscape. Lack of confidence means you might not be mentally up to the challenge or physically able to do a task. But so what; who cares? Low self-esteem centers around the emotional and psychological belief that you will fail or be ridiculed no matter what the outcome; therefore, why try at all?

It is important for parents, guardians, and teachers to instill in children a sense of positive self-esteem, reinforcement, and self-worth regardless of how small or inconsequential the acts or words. Berating, embarrassing, or pitting one child against another will not spur on the "less than" performer to try harder or rise to the challenge, but instead spawn resentment and insecurity toward not only the parent but also the sibling or friend.

Work with your child to dispense negative self-talk such as, "I can't" or "I won't be able to." If they truly can't accomplish the task, move on to something else. It's not a big deal; it's just not that person's cup of tea or strong suit. Develop something special with your child/teen that they can call their own, and you both can share in the pride of that personal growth and relationship. Young or old, we all feel good getting a pat on the back. Any effort helps strengthen an emotional bond between the one looking for approval and the one giving the approval.

Dispel mental replaying of past events that ended up in failure or were unpleasant. Participating in the blame game or keeping the embers from yesterday's experiences burning are self-destructive and reinforce to the child their inabilities to perform or meet the challenge.

It is never too late to help another with a poor self-image. One is not born with a propensity toward low self-esteem. Inappropriate or misguided comments can burrow their way under the skin and eventually into the heart and soul of one's very fiber, and this can produce a sad, scared, and lonely person.

Be there to extend a helping hand of confidence; you just may be guiding that person toward a brighter tomorrow instead of the dead end of substance abuse.

Prescription drug addiction

One would be hard-pressed to find an adult who has never taken prescription medication for physical or emotional pain. It's part of today's society to medicate what ails us. Prescription medication is designed to be easy and safe, but it can spark an addiction if not monitored. Most people in real physical or emotional pain who take prescription medication have honest and true intentions of alleviating their discomfort legally, with no intention or forethought of becoming addicted. I suffered from horrible back pain once, and when the doctors decided to administer some morphine, I certainly didn't think, "Oh boy, now I can become a drug addict legally with no repercussions."

Prescriptions are handed out today like flyers in Las Vegas. Whether you have a hangnail or an emotional hiccup, it seems that there are too many practitioners ready with their pads to prescribe any kind of antidepressant, stimulant, or muscle relaxer. Not only can your body become addicted, but your psyche and emotional senses can be dependent on such drugs as well. Sometimes a psychological addiction is more profound and more difficult to eradicate than a physical one.

Being dependent on prescription medication has nearly become acceptable addiction. Look at how many celebrities and athletes have admitted they are addicted to their painkillers for various injuries. Taking medication for sleepless nights or an old football injury are easy and plausible excuses. We tend to find ourselves saying, "Well, that's okay and understandable. Poor people, look at their lives. They are under so much pressure or pain, so it's okay." Celebrities and sports figures can still remain popular and be role models because their prescription addictions are perceived as out of their control and not intentional. The general public professes that these celebrities bring us so much joy that they are above judgment, almost immortal, and can do no wrong.

People sometimes excuse their own addictions because this or that public figure does it. Yet they and the family and friends around them know that there really is no excuse for accepting addiction to prescription medication.

Bottom line: Be careful. Everyone must be mindful to take only what they need while working a healthy rehabilitation road back from physical or emotional upheaval. Anyone who begins a drug regimen needs a plan to wean off the drug. A person with concerns about prescription addiction can enlist a support team of family and friends to help. Please note that I am not talking about monitored medication through a doctor's watchful eye, but about strong, mind-altering medication that can lead to addiction.

When experimentation turns into addiction

We have all heard people in our lives say, "Come on, don't be a chicken. Try it!" Even if we are accepted within our group of friends or trying desperately to belong, we may jump at the chance to prove our stature and worth by accepting their challenge. However, this experimental hook may present ethical, legal, or moral issues, and the outcome can result in questionable, irresponsible behavior. When the experimental challenge involves drugs or alcohol, it can lead to addiction.

Baiting and daring each other during adolescence goes with the territory. Experimentation can be construed as a rite of passage, but for our purposes the question becomes: When does experimentation turn into addiction? Experimentation turns into addiction when one can no longer walk away and the experiment has turned into a habit.

Drinking is a typical "first tier" of experimentation, holding the allure of being cool and having a good time. When teens or adolescents get a thrill out of seeing who can become the most wasted, this experimentation can quickly turn out of control and dangerous.

If this becomes any teenager's ticket to acceptance, when false "friends" eventually leave, all they are left with is a strong propensity for addiction to alcohol.

Becoming a drinker takes some work. I believe it is an acquired taste as well as feeling. I tried drinking once. I didn't like the smell, taste, or feeling, so I didn't pursue it. I wasn't interested in powering through all the discomfort to get to that happy, sloppy place that everyone seemed to enjoy.

Drugs are a different matter. People experimenting with drugs typically "shop around" to find what may satisfy them the most. One individual might be more comfortable with how cocaine makes them feel, while another relies on the amped-up feeling that methamphetamine gives them. An apt definition of experimentation is "to search out by trial or an act of experimental tests in order to determine how well something works." Drug experimentation is often a very short, direct, and dangerous path to serious problems.

Early education of children in the area of drugs and alcohol is an excellent way not only to show them we care but also to let them know we are aware of the tempting nature of experimenting with drugs and alcohol. However, please be prepared that no matter how strong your relationship is with your child and how responsible they are, or you think they are, if they want to experiment with drugs and/or alcohol there is *nothing* you can say or do that will change their mind. Experimenting isn't personally directed to you or even to dismiss or disrespect your intentions, but it's just them spreading their independent wings, right or wrong.

Most of us have our own war stories from our days of experimentation, so why not share them? A perfect opportunity to develop a tighter bond with our kids is by letting them know that we, too, faced similar challenges. Don't hold back. Find an easy, relaxed time to have an open conversation, soliciting their opinions of what they might have done differently or how they might have handled your situation. Be honest and candid. Some stories may evoke humorous memories while others might be painful, even life-altering. It might make you more human to your kids if you can let your hair down.

Encourage your teenager to have parties and friends over to your house. You can monitor from a distance as well as implement some responsible, safe rules. Trust that their parents will appreciate your

CAROLE BENNETT, M.A.

involvement and most likely the teenagers will as well. For example, make a rule that all car keys are to be kept in your possession, or have everyone make plans to spend the night. It is the wise parent who forbids any illegal drug to be part of a party scene, though impossible to police. In addition, knowing who your child or teenager hangs out with will give you an indication about their social activities.

I have often been asked if it's better for teens to drink in a supervised household than on the streets and then get behind the wheel of a car. I honestly don't have a professional opinion for that scenario; however, personally I would not allow underage drinking even though it would be in a safe and contained environment. There is a legal age for drinking, and I'm not about to break that law just because I might justify that since the kids are going to drink anyway, why not make it safe.

Growing up is all about experimentation. Whether they are experimenting about drugs, alcohol, sex, and food, or experimenting through healthy exploration such as what career path to explore, parents must make themselves as available as possible to guide and advise their children with support, love, and level-headed thinking. Try to keep the judgment at bay as much as possible. Communicate and educate early, before experimentation starts. Be available to talk and guide, but don't be afraid to intervene when and if necessary. It's more important to be a parent to our children than a pal. Addiction is easy to start, but hard to control and ultimately stop.

In all these previous paragraphs, I have listed a number of contributing factors toward addiction. You may have experienced something different with someone who has traveled a path toward an addiction to alcohol or drugs. Regardless of how one gets there, addiction is addiction, and it should be treated as dangerous and possibly life-threatening.

Please don't take lightly any of these routes that may lead to addiction, as more likely than not a light approach will come back to bite you. If you see a loved one percolating toward destructive behavior, remember that not only is the prospective addict at risk but you and your family are at risk as well. Sadly, very little cultivation is needed to take these scenarios from saplings to full-blown impervious trees that are extremely difficult to blow over or cut down.

Dispositions of relapse

In working for years with families and their loved ones' substance abuse issues, I have concluded that even though there are a myriad of reasons for relapse, there are four basic ones that can become an easy switch to flip. They are expectations, resentment, boredom, and fear. All of these represent emotional challenges for the alcoholic/addict and might represent kryptonite to some people in recovery, regardless of how long they've been sober or how strong their program. In addition, remember that maybe one or more of these dispositions might have been a major contributor to their original route to addiction in the first place.

Common dispositions of relapse:

1. **Expectations**

   Falling short of expectations or the feeling that the alcoholic/addict is unable to fulfill what is expected can open the floodgates to relapse. Whether it is your expectations as a friend or family member or the expectations of the alcoholic/addict, expectations can become unrealistic. After all, your loved one can get swept up with that initial fast or easy recovery.

   An early sense of comfort and lack of physical or emotional challenge is a honeymoon period that often falsely revolves around a happy work environment or a fairy-tale relationship. Expectations seem fulfilled at this stage, yet when the initial glow of that honeymoon subsides and reality's imperfections set in, your loved one might not know how to deal with the frustration or disappointment; hence, they may turn back to the only way they know to ensure comfort: getting high or intoxicated.

   It is crucial for the alcoholic/addict as well as the family to keep a watchful eye on their expectations. Remember that the alcoholic/addict may take on Herculean tasks in an effort to prove to themselves and others how smart, strong, or good they are, or in an attempt to make up lost time due to their addiction. Hence, they might not be able to help themselves, but will overextend in unrealistic expectations. If the expectation falls short, the alcoholic/addict may have trouble taking this failure in stride. Therefore, they may revert to the opposite end of the spectrum and find themselves saying, "I can't do anything right, so why not have a couple of snorts or belts." Falling short of expectations is a very prevalent and strong disposition for relapse.

2. **Resentment**
    When the alcoholic/addict has pent-up resentment toward a person or place, whether due to a current situation or one from twenty years ago, they can feel so overwhelmed that in order to quiet their churning resentment and anger, they feel a need to self-medicate.

    For one's recovery to be strong and potential relapse to become a non-issue, there are several roads for the person in recovery to consider in dealing with resentment. Twelve-step meetings, sponsorship, counseling, and religious or spiritual engagements are all valid support systems to help a person in recovery stay true to the desired course. Each of these options can also provide ample opportunities for venting resentments. If not resolved, resentments fester amidst the person's inner turmoil until they take the form of relapse or reckless actions.

    When I was working as an evening treatment counselor in a rehabilitation recovery program, I heard my clients say all too often that they were resentful toward a partner, family member, or institution. They got into the mind set of, "I'll show them" or "They'll be sorry," and they went out and used or drank. Keep in mind that if people with addictions have transferred old resentments that were spawned from family members or friends years ago, and they have done nothing to deal with those resentments, then they might consequently place those resentments onto an unsuspecting and innocent victim with whom they are in a current relationship.

    To you, the "normie" or "healthy one," resentments may cause a pimple or two, but usually our actions and emotions stay in check. We work through them and move on. The residual effect of resentment may produce discomfort or anger, but the outcome is rarely as detrimental as it can be for the alcoholic/addict.

    The pity-pot to the alcoholic/addict is a handy way of keeping resentments alive. Common monologues of self-pitying include statements like: "No one understands me"; "I was really dealt a bad hand"; "Nothing goes my way"; and "I'm doing the best I can, but I guess it's just not good enough."

People with addictions can find great comfort on their pity-pots, and if enough pity is allocated to them, then lo and behold, they have convinced themselves they have earned the right to drink or use. Anger fuels resentment, and resentment fuels anger. This is a vicious circle without an exit gate, and the alcoholic/addict may always find this a strong reason to justify their relapse.

Alcoholic/addicts may tend to believe their own press that tells them they are no good or are failures. They may think that their life has amounted to nothing and that they have accomplished little. Dreams and goals that they hoped for in younger days have taken a back seat due to addiction.

Often they actually resent themselves more than others for allowing this to happen. This resentment could be ongoing and perpetuate a steady buzz in the person's head; therefore, resentment presents fertile ground for relapse. Other than being open to communicating, there is nothing you can do as a family member or friend to help them deal with their resentment. Remember that some of that resentment might be about you for something you did or did not do—yesterday or even years earlier. It might be very hard for you to be impartial and difficult for your loved one to come forth with their issues, so it might not be a good idea to offer an empathetic ear.

I have had many clients report that their spouses, family members, or friends were growing more resentful toward them because they were striving and persevering in reaching their own personal goals as well as strengthening their boundaries and communication with their loved one.

Please don't allow the alcoholic/addict to clip your wings of growth, confidence, and dreams just because they are stuck on square one and, therefore, resent your determination to meet life's challenges head on. This can perpetuate the resentments that you both harbor toward each other. This does not make for an honest partnership or lend itself toward achieving the common goal of support that healthy partners should have for each other.

When I was going through my divorce, I would tell my husband that until he got rid of his resentments toward me or old resentments that he had transferred to me, we would not have a chance for reconciliation. His resentment toward me (as I pursued my dreams and goals) and his resentment toward himself (for not being able to pursue his dreams and goals) was the powder keg that I believe subconsciously blew us apart.

3. Boredom

I have already discussed boredom as a road to addiction, and it is also a disposition that leads to relapse. Boredom can lead anyone to do things they might not normally do: go on a shopping spree, gamble, eat more than usual, keep company with unsavory folks, etc. Please go back and read again the segment on boredom so you can see how insidious the action or lack of action caused by boredom can present.

4. Fear

Is the fear imagined or real? Is the fear based in reality (a head-on car collision) or rooted in the unknown? Most fear that anyone, alcoholic/addict or not, experiences is imagined. In fearing the unknown, we distrust an outcome and fear not being in control of what may or may not happen.

The alcoholic/addict might find solace in reverting to their history of fears whether it stems from childhood, adolescence, or beyond. They may be fearful of stepping outside their comfort zone as they see their results as negative or unsatisfying. This can surely impair their effort to make important changes in life.

History is a teacher, so it makes sense that if for so long the alcoholic/addict has been fearful to take chances, make uncomfortable decisions, or really face life on life's terms, then relapsing to a familiar place may be more soothing than finding themselves in a death grip of fear. They may feel that relapse and the relief of self-medicating is their only option. Sometimes the fear of better days and how to accomplish them is just too foggy and/or uncertain to pursue, so it's easier to do what is already known and comfortable, even if it's detrimental.

Common relapse triggers:

For the budding alcoholic/addict in recovery, relapse is all too often a nanosecond away. Even for the well-seasoned soul who has practiced a clean and sober lifestyle for many years, relapse may be in a dormant state or deep sleep, but it can be aroused with a touch of a feather.

In my previous book, *Reclaim Your Life: You and the Alcoholic/Addict*, I listed 77 relapse triggers—from a favorite show going off the air to getting a flat tire. If relapse is in the air, then it doesn't matter what the trigger is, the recovering alcoholic/addict will find any reason or excuse to flip the switch. However, here I list six of the most common relapse triggers.

1. **Feelings and emotions are all over the map**

    Sobriety can be a very new, oftentimes uncertain, and even scary state of mind. The alcoholic/addict has been used to living and functioning a certain way. Now all of that is gone or surely has greatly changed. We can guide and encourage our loved ones to take it slowly and understand that the body, mind, and emotions are transforming. However, the difficulty in managing these new feelings can feel so unstable to the alcoholic/addict that they quickly run out of patience to cope with this. They may believe that relapse is the only way for them to feel normal again.

2. **Difficulty living life on life's terms**

    Much like with the previous point, the alcoholic/addict in recovery has difficulty living life on life's terms. Normal, daily stressors that the "normie" or healthy one might take in stride can turn into monumental issues of a catastrophic nature for the alcoholic/addict. The alcoholic/addict's coping devices may be nonexistent or too early in their infancy, making it too hard for this person to handle dealing with the situation at hand. The alcoholic/addict may have difficulty hitting the pause button, stepping back to analyze the circumstances in a calm and clear manner, and realizing that an answer or conclusion is obtainable. In short, they may find it difficult to see that relapse does not have to be part of the equation.

    Bailing at the first sign of trouble or turning tail and heading for the hills are all too common; therefore, relapse is not only their excuse, but their answer to the problem.

3. **The staunch belief that they will never drink again**

   When the alcoholic/addict has finally committed to living a clean and sober existence, it oftentimes is like a new love affair. I have counseled many clients who spout and pontificate how they have finally realized how important sobriety is. They proudly feel that they have found the key that will halt their ever drinking again, and this very cocky nature and ego-driven thinking will almost always be their downfall. The word "humble" is missing from their vocabulary. They foolishly don't give this powerful disease the respect and caution it deserves, as they believe they are wiser and stronger than their addiction. Whether they adhere to a 12- step recovery program or not, it is the wise folks who started Alcoholics Anonymous (A.A.) long ago who staunchly state that sobriety can only be successful if taken "one day at a time."

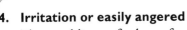

4. **Irritation or easily angered**

   The rumblings of relapse for the alcoholic/addict may find them quick to anger or more easily irritated than when practicing a clean and sober lifestyle. Your loved one could be lashing out at anyone around for no apparent reason as they find their struggle with sobriety becoming precarious. Their irritation or anger can be the result of being unable or unwilling to seek help and get the situation under check. Sometimes it takes great strength and courage to realize that they may be sinking back into that black hole, admit they are in trouble, put ego aside, and buck up to ask for help. Anger and irritation can also be mere cover-ups for feeling scared, embarrassed, or ashamed. Too many emotions going on at one time may very easily blow the circuit of sobriety, and relapse presents that doorway leading to the comfort of addiction.

5. **Loss of commitment to their recovery program**

   Rarely does the alcoholic/addict become or try to become clean and sober without help. Whether it is the Alcoholics Anonymous 12-step recovery program, outpatient or residential recovery program, or individual counseling, it is almost impossible to

IS THERE A DRY DRUNK IN YOUR LIFE? 33

self-treat years of out-of-control, abusive, addictive behavior. If relapse is knocking at your loved one's door, they may start to rearrange their sober program and use excuses for not attending A.A. meetings: "I don't need to go to this meeting; I already went to one this week. Anyway, I don't like the people there." They may make excuses for leaving a residential program early: "This place is not for me. I've gotten everything out of it there is to know." Or they may make excuses for quitting private or group counseling: "I don't like my counselor. He has no idea what I'm about and can't help me. I'm wasting my money." True and strong recovery takes years of work and is successful when coupled with an ongoing and consistent clean and sober program.

6. Hanging out with drinking buddies or visiting old haunts
There is a saying in the A.A. community: "If you visit the barber shop often enough, you're bound to get a haircut." If your loved one is starting to hang out with the old gang and visiting sites where their addiction was in full bloom, no matter how hard they try, eventually it is more likely than not they will succumb to their old ways. The alcoholic/addict may justify returning to their old friends by saying that they just want to see them or they miss them. They may swear there is no way they will indulge in any substance abuse behavior. Well, eventually that will wear thin as it stands to reason that if everyone around you is getting high, what fun are you having being clean and sober? Wanting to belong along with glamorizing and missing the good old days have a very strong pull toward relapse.

If you see these symptoms in your loved one start to rear their ugly heads, what if anything can you do about it? Honestly, very little. Remember that you cannot control whether they decide to enter a clean and sober lifestyle or continue to maintain it. You can certainly state calmly and lovingly that you have noticed a steady change in their demeanor or behavior, and you can tell them that you are concerned and are available to talk about it if they wish. If you have established consequences in the event of a relapse, you can certainly remind them of what's at stake if they continue down this possibly destructive path.

Please keep in mind that you are not the cause and not responsible if there is a relapse. They may try to rope you in or pin it on you in some way, but the bottom line is that their commitment to live a clean and sober lifestyle rests solely and squarely on their shoulders.

Relapse can take on many shapes and forms. The important thing is not *what form* the relapse takes, or even *why* one relapses, but rather deciding *how* one will change and, therefore, commit to a stronger, more formidable recovery program in the future.

What can the alcoholic/addict learn from a misstep? Relapse doesn't have to be a hanging offense. You want to keep in mind all the previous clean and sober days. I've had many clients tell me that the relapse wasn't so bad, that it was just one or two drinks and not several cases of beer or three bottles of wine. I once heard from a recovering alcoholic that "one drink is too many and a thousand is never enough." So relapse is relapse no matter how you paint it.

The route of recovery can be a very circuitous path. Be mindful that at the end of the day, only the person recovering from addiction knows how strong their commitment to their recovery program is, and only they know whether they are practicing recovery or relapse.

Processing Questionnaire

- Who in your life has a substance abuse issue?

- How long have you suspected such and why?

- What actions have you taken?

- Is there a friend or another member of the family who agrees with your concern and is a participant in their everyday life?

- What is your plan to confront this situation?

- What are your plans for getting professional advice (not just going to an Al-Anon meeting or asking a friend over lunch) as to how to proceed?

CHAPTER 3

WHEN IS IT TIME TO THROW
IN THE TOWEL?

Deciding to walk away from a relationship is usually a difficult decision. In a conventional scenario it can be tough enough, but add in the element of substance abuse and there can be added stress.

With an addiction landscape there may come a time when you feel that you have exhausted all your avenues in trying to live with your mate's substance abuse issues and your own personal wellbeing is now in danger. You have run out of gas, and the only healthy option is to throw in the towel and make a dramatic, earthshaking move.

Like the alcoholic/addict who may hit bottom before realizing that it's time to change the course of their life, or die, you as the family member or friend can hit bottom as well. With months or even years of weighing this gut-wrenching decision, it can finally culminate from anger to frustration to sheer exhaustion. Either way, you have probably shed buckets of tears and can't believe that your life has come to this fork in the road.

I know that when I decided to leave my husband because of his addictive behavior, I spent what seemed to be a decade of sleepless nights pondering my decision. After all, regardless of his disposition, I did love the man, we had a family, and after twenty years had built a life together, but deep down I knew I had to bail. I didn't know who I was anymore. Like someone drowning, I was desperate to grab on to any piece of wood that might allow me to reclaim my life. Despite the excruciating pain that I knew would accompany my decision, I had to believe it would be better in the long run for myself and my family. I kept in mind that the big picture of making a new life had to outweigh the almost impossibility that tomorrow would be different if I stayed. I had been down that disappointing road so many times before that I found it helpful to burn those memories in my head since I knew I would call upon them in the future when I felt shaky about my decision.

14 reasons why one stays in a relationship with the alcoholic/addict longer than they should:

1. You are gripped with fear as to what life might be.

2. You feel your children are better off with two parents rather than one, regardless of the discomfort and tension in the household.

3. You worry about being financially compromised because the alcoholic/addict is the chief money-maker.

4. You have a fear of retribution.

5. You have a fear of being alone.

6. You are hanging on to the few shreds of normal behavior that the alcoholic/addict randomly shows (and continuing to hope that one day it might stick).

7. You feel social, family (extended or otherwise), and peer pressure are telling you to keep trying to stick it out.

8. You believe that if you "do this" or "do that" things will change.

9. You think that the alcoholic/addict's problems are because you "didn't do this" or "didn't do that."

10. You feel embarrassed and ashamed.

11. You worry about what people will say and about the gossip.

12. You made a commitment or have religious constraints.

13. You think the relationship a poor reflection on self and self-esteem.

14. You don't want to be perceived as a failure as a parent or spouse.

14 reasons that might propel you to make a difficult but life-saving decision:

1. You are mentally and physically exhausted in dealing with the alcoholic/addict's out-of-control behavior.

2. You can no longer trust what the alcoholic/addict says or does.

3. You are fed up with the alcoholic/addict who continues to bully, ridicule, disrespect, and blame you for their shortcomings and failures.

4. You are weary of the constant merry-go-round of rehabilitation attempts that don't seem to stick for long.

5. You will feel actually embarrassed for yourself if you stay one more minute.

6. You are unable to recognize yourself anymore and wonder where you went.

7. You realize that you deserve better.

8. You are no longer fearful of being alone, and you realize that you are already alone since the alcoholic/addict is living a life apart from you with their drug of choice.

9. You see that everyone's world is revolving around the alcoholic/addict; consequently, other family members may be suffering.

10. You are fearful of any communication and find yourself walking on eggshells in an effort to not engage their anger.

11. You are convinced that no matter how hard you try, the alcoholic/addict will keep raising the bar for you to "do your part" in the relationship; satisfaction is never reached.

12. You sense that the thought of spending one more minute of your life like this is beginning to make you physically ill.

13. You no longer care how it looks to others, what anyone says, or what the ramifications may be of your decision; you have the exit gate in your sights.

14. You look and feel awful. Your work and hobbies are suffering as well as relationships with family members or friends.

If you have indeed hit your bottom and are ready to take the painful but appropriate step to move on with your life without the alcoholic/addict, please don't beat yourself up for not having acted on this resolve sooner. Other than the list mentioned above, people stay in unhealthy relations substantially longer than they should or know that they should. It is very hard to blow out the candle in the window that might represent hope, but realistically, you know it doesn't offer true hope at all. Try and remember that a few years of discomfort, uncertainty, and fear are better than years and years of an agonizing and miserable commitment.

Restricting your relationships

We have talked about the reasons why we can't or won't break away from the dry drunk or alcoholic/addict and why we should. Let's take a minute to talk about other people in our lives. Your relationship issues with the alcoholic/addict may have put strain on some of your other relationships. Also, along with changing your relationship with the alcoholic/addict, you may feel it's time to change other relationships as well.

So what does it look like to throw in the towel with the not-so-nice person or the person you just don't like but at one time you considered a friend? It's oftentimes painful to abandon a friendship. You have probably put a lot of time and energy into your relationships, but what if one has run its course? Perhaps it wasn't the friendship that it was at one time or wasn't really the friendship you thought it was. Maybe your standards or views on things have changed, or maybe you have just grown apart from this person.

The following is a list of some relationship traits that we just can't get behind or forgive or get past, or, or, or . . .

Negative karma

It is very difficult to be around someone who is always complaining, negative, or in a sour mood, especially if that person talks about their woes incessantly. No matter how hard we try to be empathetic and listen, we find ourselves tuning out from the drone of negative energy. Our state of mind, no matter how positive or upbeat will quickly be shrouded with a cloud of yuck from the infection of the person's crummy attitude and outlook on life. This is not a friend we want to keep.

Always sick

I had a friend who was always sick. He was not seriously ill, but he always had one thing or another wrong. If it wasn't his headaches, then it was his stomach or legs. I tried desperately to be understanding with each ailment, until he started bailing at the last minute when we had plans made weeks in advance. I lost patience, so there went the friendship.

A friendship with no substance

All of our friends bring different energies. Some friends we have because we enjoy their smarts. With some we enjoy their love of life. Friends make us laugh, think, or whatever. But sometimes we find ourselves in a friendship that has no substance, a boring, shallow relationship that has peaked in twenty minutes of getting together. Life is too short to be keeping company with someone who adds zero to your life.

One-sided friendship

You give and give, but nothing comes back. A one-sided friendship can be the most frustrating, impersonal relationship around. This person has a tough time in merely saying, "Thank you" or "What can I do for you?" You don't want to column-keep a friendship, but when you do all the work in keeping the friendship fresh and productive, it's probably time to find a new friend.

Combative, know it all

It's no fun to be with someone who is combative, argumentative, or knows it all. Every comment sparks a raised eyebrow or a debate from the weather to current events. Your opinion holds no worth and is summarily dismissed as if you are an idiot.

Always late

Personally, I can't stand someone who is always late. Once or twice with a text or phone call that says there is traffic or that an emergency popped up is certainly not a problem. But when someone is consistently late, in essence they are saying that your time is not valuable and they will show when it's convenient for them.

Rarely apologizes or takes responsibility for their own mistakes

Why is saying "I'm sorry" so difficult for many people? An apology that is then connected to a defend-and-justify posture is at best a half-hearted one. "I'm sorry, but . . . " does not count in my book. On the same token, one that has difficulty apologizing might find it equally hard to take responsibility for some questionable actions, great or small.

Poor follow through

Trust is a main component in any relationship. It is difficult to have a sincere friendship with someone who doesn't keep their word or has spotty commitments to you. This person can often leave you hanging when you are waiting for an answer regarding plans or getting together. We feel so uncomfortable when we have to dog another person for an answer to a proposed get together. Like being constantly late, it's a quiet slap in the face, showing no or little respect for the other person.

Your views and opinions are at opposite ends of the spectrum

Politics and religion are always topics people say to stay away from. If you have a friendship with someone who spends most of your time together trying to convert you to their religion, or your friend just plainly doesn't like dogs when they mean the world to you, then the relationship might be challenged or tense. You don't need to delete them from your phone list, but you might find spending less time with them to be more comfortable for both of you.

The bottom line is that these relationships are unpleasant or uncomfortable, and we could do better by eradicating them from our lives. People are there to enrich our lives, not make us feel uncomfortable, sad, or empty. We want to be there for our friends, but we should make sure they are really friends who would be there for us too.

Here's a good way to calculate when it's time to fish or cut bait with this person. When you see their number or name show up on your phone or computer and you duck the call more than three times, it's time to put that relationship on hiatus or in the recycle bin.

What about family members? It's a sad realization when you realize you just don't like some or many of them. Every year around the holidays I do an emotional housekeeping of friends and family. The older I get, the more I find that my time is precious and my own company sometimes is more enjoyable than being with others.

Nancy's story

I had a client who shared that she was confused and disappointed in some of the family members and friends who were participating in the Thanksgiving dinner. Though no one was intoxicated or high, she realized that she left with an unsettled, almost empty feeling about the evening. It took her a few days to sift through her emotional discomfort and put some kind of description or label on what she had experienced and how it was affecting her.

Nancy's communication to me was cloaked with a sense of embarrassment as she sadly realized that she didn't like the way some of her family members and purported friends had acted over this holiday season. They were loud, obnoxious, opinionated, dictatorial, and downright rude. Even when things seemed to settle down or unwind from the hectic preparation and conclusion of the evening, no one asked her how she was doing or about what was new in her life. Nancy was recently divorced from an alcoholic and venturing on a new career, and she hadn't seen some of her family members for quite some time. She had been hopeful that the reunion and subsequent conversations would be warm, genuine, and gentle and not one of manic, herky-jerky discussions and actions.

As she sat back and pretended she was invisible, scoping out the room and its inhabitants from a corner, she saw her family acted like wind-up toys on helium. Nancy felt badly that she was judging them. Yet, with all the work she was doing to rid herself of the toxic man in her life, her need to detox was inadvertently spilling over into relationships with other members of her family.

Emotional housekeeping

It's important to do emotional housekeeping as an honest way to take care of a healthier self on a frequent basis. If you choose to do this inventory, ask yourself what some of the guidelines or prerequisites would be for that person to stay a complementary part of your life.

Maybe you want to take a second look at some of these people who have become like a pebble in your shoe. You might realize that you don't want to have these family members around quite as much. There's nothing wrong with that. This doesn't have to mean eradicating them from your life, just making some healthy changes. Remember, you can always go back to your old habits and ways, but how will you know if it could be better unless you try something new?

8 signs that this is a person you need to detox from your life:

1. Giving off bad vibes or energy

2. Leaving you emotionally drained

3. Leaving you questioning yourself

4. Making you feel "less than"

5. Bullying you

6. Not encouraging you

7. Placating you

8. Constantly judging you

12 behaviors that tell you a person is toxic in your life:

1. You know the person doesn't really like you but just pretends to because you are family or connected in some way.

2. From conversations and what others tell you, you know this person is two-faced.

3. The person inevitably does not keep their word.

4. This person seems to always find fault with you and frequently challenges the decisions you make in your life.

5. You know the person talks badly about you behind your back, feigns concern about you, and offers "expertise" to help you, but then is annoyed if you rebuff the invitation or advice.

6. You and others can no longer ignore how often the this person shouts at you or speaks to you disrespectfully.

7. This person never asks you how you are doing or expresses true concern for you. This person doesn't really care about what you have gone through, doesn't respect who you really are, and isn't interested in what your hopes and dreams are for tomorrow.

8. You know they still blame you for disappointing or sad experiences from the past and are not interested in listening to you or understanding why these events happened.

9. They want your company one minute, and then *poof!* . . . You're snubbed until they need you for something again.

10. This person does nothing but take, and rarely if ever gives back.

11. They want you listen to their woes, but they don't have time to listen to what is on your mind.

It is sad, scary, disappointing, and unnerving to come to the realization that you just don't like some people you have spent much of your life trying to love. However, you can love them and accept them while realizing their limitations. Don't set yourself up with expectations for anything to change. Realize that just because you have bought them special gifts, played with their children, or cleaned up their kitchen that their relationship with you will improve. How they treat you may not ever change, for whatever reason.

4 ways to protect yourself from fangs and claws before going into the proverbial lions' den:

1. Schedule to spend a minimum amount of time with the friend or family member. Don't hope that things might be different. If they are, then great, it's an added bonus. If you have a good get-together, don't take it to the bank that they have changed or that it will be like this from now on.

2. Have an exit plan to cut short a visit that might go badly. For example, before visiting her daughter, my client learned the train schedule and didn't commit to a definite return time.

3. Remind yourself that they are responsible for their actions, not you. Please, please don't lose sleep wondering what you did or didn't do to that family member to make them act this way.

4. Come home to a four-legged friend wagging its tail or purring in your lap—this is the very best of the best.

If you aren't dependent upon these people, then you'll find it freeing when you finally take a deep breath and are honest with yourself about their place in your life. You don't need to share this new emotional freedom with anyone as "loose lips sink ships." There is no need to get anyone in your corner to agree with you or make you feel like you have to defend and justify your position. Consider this your chance to do emotional housekeeping for any season of the year when you want to get the broom and dustpan out.

Self-toxic

We've spent some time talking about the other people in our lives who might not warrant our friendship, but what about us? What if we are toxic to ourselves? Sometimes we can't get out of our own way or protect ourselves from ourselves. We can be self-degrading, impatient, even dismissive of our efforts. We can truly be our own worst enemy. All the energy, love, accomplishments, and dreams that we hold dear can vanish in a second if we let that inner voice of negativity get to us.

It's difficult to stand up for yourself or be strong in your convictions when you don't believe them yourself. It's hard to tell a friend or family member when they are overstepping their boundaries with you if you have no idea what your boundaries are.

Honest inner strength comes with time, effort, and loads of practice at saying no and being true to you. Don't go somewhere if you don't want to. Don't say things that you don't mean if they're only meant to make someone else happy or not make waves. Make those waves! Maybe it's time for you to discover who you are. When you stand up for yourself, you will find that you not only like yourself but respect yourself quite a bit as well. You'll only be sorry that it took you this long to discover a pretty cool you.

I discuss in chapter 12 how to move on with your life. Not only can you relinquish the hold that the alcoholic/addict, friends, or family members may have on you but also you can remove the emotional devil that's inside of you, the one that is constantly saying you are not good enough and not capable enough to pursue a better, healthier life and lifestyle. Hogwash! Trust me, it's there. I'm a breathing, walking example of the once shrinking violet that turned into a bird of prey!

Processing Questionnaire

- Is it time to throw in the towel?

- If so, with whom? If you're throwing in the towel in your struggle with the alcoholic/addict, please carefully read about the recovery contract (chapter 6). If the person is your spouse, be aware that this is not as easy as it would be with a friend or family member.

- Why are you throwing in the towel?

- What does the plan look like if you want to restrict your relationship? (Fewer phone calls a week, fewer lunches, verbal boundaries that you want to discuss, etc.)

- Are you scared to make changes? If so, why?

- Are you ready to try?

CHAPTER 4

IS IT IMPORTANT TO SEEK OUTSIDE HELP?

Every person who is dealing with a loved one's prospective or full-blown addiction issue wrings their hands with fear, frustration, and a boatload of unanswered questions.

- How did this happen?

- Was I blind to this problem?

- What should I do?

- Whom should I call?

These are natural concerns that understandably keep us up at night. Our first stop for outside help is usually family and friends, but maybe not if we feel embarrassed or ashamed. In the case of this being your child you are concerned about, and if there is a fairly strong family bond, then certainly it is your spouse who is first on board with the what, where, when, why, and how.

I have often suggested (strongly, I might say) to my clients to not engage friends or even go for help outside the core family unit. *Everyone* will have a different opinion or viewpoint as what to do or how to proceed to help the alcoholic/addict in question. Undoubtedly, your head will spin with "do this" or "do that." Though they may even have had similar situations in their own family or know someone who has traveled the same path, their advice may not work for you. All circumstances are different since all family dynamics are different.

What might have worked for one person close to you might not work for another person you know. A wilderness or rigid back-to-nature recovery program might be perfect for one teen, but another teen might need comforting and tender surroundings. Do your own research and talk to a professional addiction counselor or therapist. In the case of a child or young adult still in school or college, talk to one of the guidance counselors for some unfettered advice. If your son or daughter is beyond school years and is living at home waiting to find what's next on the agenda, that's a different story, in which case the responsibility of recovery falls more into their own lap than yours.

Knowledge is power. The place I have found incredibly helpful with my family's addiction issues and the very first place I suggest to my clients is an open Alcoholics Anonymous (A.A.) meeting. Since so many people attend these meetings, you should plan to get to the meeting early to find a seat for yourself.

8 reasons why I champion an open A.A. meeting as the first step for seeking outside help:

1. Attending an open A.A. meeting means just that. It is open for anyone who wants to attend whether they have an addiction issue or not.

2. In this typically 90-minute meeting, there are speakers who talk briefly about their paths of addiction and recovery.

3. At each meeting there is a main speaker with many years of recovery under their belt who talks about what life was like as an addict, their numerous times of relapse and recovery, and what their life is like clean and sober and living life on life's terms.

4. You don't have to say a word.

5. It's free.

6. The camaraderie between those in recovery is moving and stimulating.

7. You are not alone.

8. Most importantly, you will hear that there is hope, that many have traveled the same trek, and that they survived and came out the other side better, stronger, and healthier.

The worst thing you can do is come away feeling more depressed than when you walked through the door. This is the reality of the world of addiction and recovery. You should understand how it works from the folks who know it only too well. The other thing that won't work is saying, "*Phew!* My child isn't as bad off as these people. I'm obviously overreacting." Better you not attend than that you live in denial that addiction is unhealthy for you and your loved one.

This is not about signing them up to go to the meeting with you or even suggesting to them that they should try it out. This is for you and your education. It has nothing to do with them. This is an early step in seeking outside help without committing to anything.

Many family members and friends dealing with their loved one's addiction issues attend Al-Anon meetings. Al-Anon is a 12-step recovery program that is the counterpart to the Alcoholics Anonymous 12-step recovery program. It was initiated by Lois Wilson, wife of Bill Wilson, one of the original founders of Alcoholics Anonymous, as a safe haven and support group for anyone dealing with a loved one's alcoholism and/or drug addiction.

For years I attended Al-Anon meetings. Yet I had come away from my first meeting thinking, "What a bunch of losers." As well, I knew I had heard some interesting things there. I encourage my clients to attend Al-Anon coupled with the open A.A. meetings to find out if these meetings are something they wish to incorporate in their recovery. Some swear by it, while others have no interest.

8 hip-hip hoorays for Al-Anon:

1. A unique camaraderie of people coming together in a safe forum for a common interest. No one cares what you wear or if you have money or a job. We are all in the same boat, sharing the same theme of addiction hardships.

2. A neutral approach that is nonjudgmental toward others, yet personal enough to share some deep-seated fears and concerns.

3. Often meetings are held in church social rooms. This is comforting in its serenity, which may elicit a feeling of being spiritually content.

4. The Al-Anon literature is expressive and powerful. Many Al-Anon members start their day reading from *One Day at a Time* or *Courage to Change*. These readings can be a lifeline for someone struggling with a certain issue in which that daily reading may shed some encouragement.

5. Attending Al-Anon regularly and experiencing other people's growth and progress can increase your own buoyancy. You may witness members' emotional failures and successes, and you are likely to feel empowered by their accomplishments and applaud them for "hanging in there."

6. Sharing your own failures and successes with others who are struggling or new to the program is amazingly satisfying. Becoming a sponsor helps you to continue in your recovery while helping others. A sponsor is someone who has clocked a sufficient amount of time in the A.A./Al-Anon program to help others with readings, concepts, and step-work.

7. The importance of a Higher Power in your life is tantamount to a successful recovery. Al-Anon readings and sharings are overflowing with reference to a Higher Power and turning our will over to that Higher Power and trusting in the results. For many (including myself), it is very comforting to have a "silent partner" who is always watching out for my best interests even if I can't see them for myself.

8. There is no membership fee; however, it is customary to donate a dollar at a meeting (if you can afford it). Every group is supposed to be self-supporting and the donations help pay for the rent and the books.

8 bah humbugs about Al-Anon:

1. At the meetings, people "air their dirty laundry" for all to see. It's nobody's business what goes on behind closed doors. Why would a person present a vulnerable image of themselves or their family as failures? ("I live in this community . . . what if I see someone I know . . . maybe my family/friends will be angry or embarrassed that I am attending these meetings.")

2. Hearing other people's stories can lead to denial about being in a destructive and dangerous situation. ("My qualifier [the loved one struggling with a substance abuse issue] isn't nearly as bad as some others"; "I'm not as sad/angry/frustrated like so many of these other people in the room. I don't really need this program.")

3. It's difficult to face the realization that one's own life may be out of control due to the alcoholic/addict and that something has to be done about it. The family member or friend may not want to participate in the heavy lifting of change and the discomfort experienced in the beginning in order to establish new boundaries and self-respect. It may seem easier to bump along the bottom than commit to new thinking.

4. Some members of Al-Anon take themselves way too seriously, and this can be a turn off to members. Like any organization, A.A. needs to have rules and regulations; however, it is unnecessary to admonish someone for sharing about a book or an article they read that relates to their share, or for acknowledging someone's comments in your own share with a glance and being accused of crosstalk. If someone thinks they are doing it "wrong," they might be more hesitant to be open and honest.

5. Some members use Al-Anon as a soap box, a self-serving forum to drone on and on about personal problems that have no relevance to the program. They justify this by adding a disclaimer at the end of their diatribe that they would not be able to say this or do that if Al-Anon had not been in their life.

6. Members who have no religious affiliation may find discomfort in any type of greater being or holier-than-thou entity, especially if it means "turning their will and care over to a Higher Power" in order to achieve success.

7. Some feel that the emphasis on a Higher Power and the greatness of the Al-Anon program comes almost to the point of sounding like a cult.

8. Many people who attend Al-Anon say it takes *years* to finally "get it." One must be dedicated to attend meetings frequently and work with a sponsor before they can feel fairly secure in their own recovery. Many are not interested in investing so much time. And honestly . . . what do they "get"? And how do they know they've "got it"?

For a long time, Al-Anon was an enormous help to me. After a time, I got tired of the same old ritual, the same people sharing. Frankly, I was bored to tears. Because one is not allowed to share or exchange views, offer advice, or do anything other than pat the back of the person next to them, I came to find these meetings unfulfilling and tedious.

I don't want to throw the Al-Anon program totally under the bus since it's a great way for people to know they are not alone and have many of the same situations brewing right down the street from them. Sharing the trials and tribulations of loving an alcoholic/addict and seeing Al-Anon folks nodding their heads in agreement assures everyone that they are not alone. This presents a very special bond that transcends the norm of most friendships.

Al-Anon is surely worth a try, and like everything new, it takes time. Above all else, keep an open mind. As they say in the meetings, "Take what you like and leave the rest." Since I am a family substance abuse counselor, it goes without saying that I strongly believe that if one has the opportunity to seek one-on-one guidance, it can be an essential way to process feelings and options. Be mindful that going to a marriage and family therapist is not the same as seeing a specialist in substance abuse counseling. It's like going to a family practitioner for an eye or pelvic exam.

I rarely see recovering alcoholics or addicts in my practice because I think there are many sources available to them. I specialize in working with the families. However, I often see the alcoholic/addict in conjunction with their spouse or parents. This way, when we discuss the family recovery contract and each other's expectations, everyone is on the same page and not guessing what the rules and regulations are within the family.

The bottom line is that a family member should not deal with their loved one's addiction issues on their own. Reading books and researching answers online is helpful, but trusting a professional who has traveled a similar path is important and of far greater value. Don't get bogged down with so many books that your head is spinning about which advice to take and which advice to ignore.

In addition, talking to friends, work associates, and neighbors is not recommended since this can put some unnecessary stress on your relationships. Also, outside advice should be taken carefully since what might have worked for them may not work for you. There is nothing to be ashamed of if a loved one has an addiction issue, but it still is a private and tender subject that should be kept in the family and shared only with appropriate people.

Processing Questionnaire

- What outside resources are you exploring?

- Are these resources helpful? If so, why? If not so, why not?

- What is your time frame on seeking and using outside help?

- What do you think about the open A.A. meeting?

- When do you plan to go to an open A.A. meeting?

- If you've attended an open A.A. meeting, will you go again?

- Is attending an Al-Anon meeting helpful? If so, why? If not so, why not?

CHAPTER 5

WHY IS THE ALCOHOLIC/ADDICT SO SELF-DESTRUCTIVE?

If I have heard it once, I have heard it a thousand times, "Why did this relapse happen when everything was going so well?" It's a common hue and cry. Honestly, I have no concrete answer, only suppositions. Even with my own husband (now ex), I heard myself posing the same question to my dogs. They didn't have an answer either.

So what motivates an individual to purposely put an invisible, destructive gun to their head and pull the trigger time and time again? As "normies" or healthy ones, we can't imagine how anyone can go down such a path that would deliberately obliterate everything that we hold so near and dear.

3 thoughts to ponder as to why the alcoholic/ addict goes down that road:

1. Sometimes when alcoholics start to get a handle on their recovery, or the going gets too good, they sabotage it. Though they freely admit that they are healthier and feel better, this new way of life can feel unfamiliar and uncomfortable no matter how hard they try accepting a clean, sober, and enjoyable lifestyle. It's exceptionally hard for someone to shake old habits, thoughts, and actions. For so long they have known one way, a destructive path, but an oddly familiar and comfortable one nonetheless.

2. They might have difficulty trusting that their new life is good, that they've earned it and worked hard to get there, and that

this way will continue to remain good so long as they stay on a clean and sober path. Alcoholic/addicts may not feel they deserve some of the good things that are happening to them, and this can be at the root of their self-sabotage. In addition, the expectations of others that they will "keep up the good work" can be a lot of pressure. Too often they retreat into what's familiar with the slightest hiccup or a continued barrage of hiccups (whether real or imagined), even when they know that the familiar crutch will be detrimental or may produce substantial wreckage. The ups and downs of life that the normie experiences and can work through are seen as monumental hurdles to the alcoholic/addict. Life on life's terms can be so daunting and overwhelming that their thinking tells them to bail at whatever cost.

3. They are not getting the attention they used to when they were struggling with their addiction. Everything and everyone around them has returned to normal, and they are no longer the subject or object of everyone's hand-wringing. No matter what their age, they find it more fun to act like a child again, to stir the pot, so to speak. Remember that negative attention is better than no attention at all.

Moira's story

I had been working with a client for many months whose story I found important enough to share, with her permission. Moira divorced her alcoholic husband (Mark) a few years ago. She didn't leave the marriage because she fell out of love, but because she could no longer deal with the baiting and punishing, dry drunk behavior, and steady stream of relapse and recovery. As was becoming their pattern, they would reconnect when he was about six-months clean and sober, but she had specific boundaries that she had firmly implemented and which kept her comfortable within the relationship.

She enjoyed his company, and like in most long-term relationships, they had a lot in common and, of course, a special history. For the last several months he had been living at a sober living house. He had become one of the managers and, therefore, had been granted a small salary and room and board. He also had another job that he loved very much. She saw him three times a week, and things were calm, fun, and loving.

However, her ex wanted to move back in and insisted that they head in that direction, or he would either ask for a transfer to another location from one of his jobs or start dating others. She told him that there was no way he was going to move back in since they had done that dance without success for several years, besides she enjoyed the relationship as it was. He proclaimed that she was selfish, but his barbs rolled off her back as she was firmly committed to what was healthy and working for her.

It wasn't long until things started to unravel for him. Instead of Mark hitting the pause button and deciding in a mature way whether he wanted to keep the relationship on the level it was on or sadly move on, he put together a plan (whether consciously or not) that would be horribly self-destructive.

In addition, his place of work ratcheted back his hours since he was not available for the hours they needed, for he worked those as manager of his sober living house. Instead of quitting his job at the sober living facility and finding an apartment so he could open himself up for more hours at this other job, Moira and I concluded that he relapsed so he would be kicked out of sober living and be forced to get an apartment. In addition, Mark rode his almost brand new scooter after he'd been drinking. As a result, he damaged it and received a DUI (his second). Mark knew that Moira would be disgusted by this unbelievably stupid behavior and not want to see him anymore.

When this first happened, she couldn't help but email him and ask him why he hadn't left the scooter safely parked somewhere and walk or take a cab to a hotel before he tied one on. Then the damage would have been only a relapse; whereas now, he had a suspended license for God knows how many years and thousands of dollars in fines and legal fees. Of course, she received no response from him.

She did receive a text that said, "Don't give up on me; I haven't." Her response was that she couldn't give him an answer since she had never met anyone so personally self-destructive in her life.

For weeks she shook her head on the unbelievable stupidity of this relapse, and then she realized sadly that she couldn't trust or be friends with someone with so little respect for themselves. She had come to the end of whatever relationship they had, and surprisingly she wasn't upset. She reminded herself of a favorite consoling quote that she often turned to in times of uncertainty: "Sometimes God does for us what we can't do for ourselves."

Maybe it was time for the friendship to be over, but neither one of them could really put the brakes on. Maybe she would not have been able to meet someone else unless Mark was completely out of her life. And maybe Mark needed to eradicate himself from her in order to move on. Who knows, and only time will tell.

Moira prays for his peace and sobriety and hopes that one day he finds his comfort zone and can love himself with respect and dignity.

It's not "all your fault"

It's important to understand that your loved one makes a personal decision on whether to stay clean and sober or to relapse. You have zero part in it. Don't let yourself get roped into taking any of the blame for the relapse. You don't have that much power over another individual. We all sail our own ship. The alcoholic/addict may justify their plan of self-sabotage by roping you into the scenario. Comments like, "It's all your fault"; or "You won't do what I need you to"; or "I'll show you"; or my favorite, "You'll be sorry."

Deep down inside they may realize that using you as a dart board for their actions is ridiculous, and that they alone are responsible for their own proceedings. However, pointing the finger at someone else as the catalyst for this reckless behavior makes it palatable and gives them fuel to follow through with their intentions.

As normies we can't help but shake our heads when we learn of a relapse after our loved ones were clean and sober for so long and seemingly had a handle on their sobriety. I have found myself saying both professionally and personally, "You've got to be kidding . . . another relapse? How amazingly stupid!" Stupidity and relapse seem to go hand in hand. It seems that there are countless stories of one's loved one tripping over themselves to self-sabotage their life with relapse after relapse.

Guilt is not part of this dance. It is a solo act, and no one other than the alcoholic/addict is responsible for their actions and decisions. They fall on their sword or rise like a phoenix, but it's up to them and *only* them.

I believe that the alcoholic/addict knows when they are on the road to self-sabotage. They know that their behavior will result in substantial and probable irreparable damage. Their credibility, accountability, reliability, and dependability will be shot to hell. Yet like a car out of control, they can't bring themselves to hit the brakes or pull to the side of the road to regroup.

When my husband and I were still married, he attended anywhere from three to five A.A. meetings a week. He professed that he and his sponsor were on the same page, and he in turn sponsored some new members. So when he relapsed I would ask him why he didn't call his sponsor for help when the urge to relapse came over him. His answer was so flippant and contrite I couldn't believe it. He said, "If I call him, he will talk me out of drinking." I shook my head in disbelief and wondered why he had a sponsor to begin with.

If you are in a relationship with someone who is hell-bent on playing Russian roulette with self-sabotage, know that there is absolutely nothing you can do about it. You will drive yourself crazy trying to appease. Moving locales, expanding your family, or switching from Republican to Democrat will not change anything; or if it does, it's only for a brief time. It's solely and completely up to the alcoholic/addict to take and keep control of their life, whether in a strong and resilient recovery program or the slippery slope of relapse and self-destruction.

Being with someone who has such strong self-destructive tendencies is like living with someone with anger displacement or who is very moody. You have no idea which disposition will take charge of the day. Just when you think you have had a perfectly wonderful day, no arguments, sun shining, intimacy, and a yummy meal, the alcoholic/addict says that they need to go for a bit, and before long they are intoxicated like the old days.

What happened? Who knows? The world of addiction is like knowing what life is like on Mars—foreign and impossible to figure out, so don't try. You can either adjust your life accordingly to their lifestyle or run for the hills.

Processing Questionnaire

- How many relapses has your loved one had?

- What has been the outcome of those relapses?

- What is the disposition of the alcoholic/addict today?

- What action have you taken because of these relapses?

- What does the future look like for you after another relapse?

CHAPTER 6

WHY ARE THE RECOVERY CONTRACT, BOUNDARIES, AND EXPECTATIONS IMPORTANT?

Of all the chapters and columns I have written, nothing is more important than implementing a family recovery contract. After the hard work you have done processing the chapters in this book, all will be for naught if you have no *recovery plan*! You will find that I repeat some of these concepts more than once, looking at it from a few different points of view. I want to make sure you are crystal clear on all aspects of the recovery plan.

Start your recovery contract or plan by stating that leaving the program early is not an option. I have heard time and time again how the alcoholic/addict decided on their own that they didn't need to complete the required amount of days/months or that this program was not for them. Unless there is a bona fide reason for such (their wellbeing may be in jeopardy or the population is dangerous), don't buy into their thinking that they know best. As they say in A.A., their stinkin' thinkin' got them there to begin with.

The recovery contract

A recovery plan is just that: A plan for those in recovery and those associated with recovery to incorporate realistic goals and consequences if one falls short of those goals.

It is the irresponsible parent, spouse, family member, or friend who does not insist upon a structure or plan, and instead hopes that everything will work out okay or that a few well-intended ideas from the alcoholic/addict will suffice.

You may start out with good and clear intentions of what you expect from the alcoholic/addict as they begin to put their life back together, but we all struggle with what to do next if those goals or expectations are not met. Verbal commitments *do not work!* They are forgotten or misinterpreted, and unlike a written piece of paper, no one can go back and check the details.

You don't want to babysit the alcoholic/addict; however, if they are living under your roof, they must live within your guidelines. Both parties need to have already agreed to the stipulations and consequences that come with the privilege of living in someone else's house.

I have heard many clients say that their son or daughter returned to live at home after being involved in a recovery program and that the family requested or even demanded that they keep their room clean, return to school, get a job, or help with the household chores. Their child agreed, but everyone slacked off after awhile; family and friends got busy or things were rolling along with hit and miss results, and everyone became complacent, and frankly too lazy, to stop a slow-moving train toward relapse. When this occurred, I would ask my clients what happened to their agreement on consequences.

I'm going to discuss two different recovery plans, one for a child who might be still under the umbrella of their family and one for an adult, whether a friend, sibling, or spouse. As long as the alcoholic/addict is in recovery and your life is involved with theirs, this plan represents important boundaries and guidelines that not only will help the recovering alcoholic/addict to stay honest and present but also will develop respect between them and you.

It is important to tackle this recovery contract *together* and in writing *before* they come home. It doesn't do any good to have your loved one home for a few days or weeks and then implement a plan. Don't wait until the horse is out of the barn. The plan doesn't have the effect it should have once their suitcase is unpacked or they are comfortable in their already established living situation. With that said, have the alcoholic/addict put together what they see as *their* recovery plan first!

Writing a recovery contract

Let's take a look at how you might go about writing a plan for someone who states they want to get a job or would like to do volunteer work to fill their time.

- Have them write down what they want to see happen (get a full-time job, attend school as a full-time student, etc.).

- Have them write down how they see this happening, (Internet, personally going into establishments, etc.).

- Have them state their time frame for securing a job or volunteer work (ten days, two weeks, etc.).

- Have them write down what they agree are reasonable consequences if they don't find a job or volunteer work within that time (allowance suspended, no cell phone use, etc.).

Be careful not to be too vague. For example, you want to implement that the recovering alcoholic/addict be home at a reasonable hour. Pinpoint a specific time; don't just leave it to a last minute decision or whatever the alcoholic/addict thinks is reasonable. Another example is that you insist the alcoholic/addict's room is kept neat. Does this mean a "white glove" cleanliness or just clothes off the floor? Again, be specific; leave nothing to interpretation!

Basic 4-point recovery contract

Pick the four most important areas that you want to see included in the recovery plan. More than four areas is too much to monitor and could be too much for their budding recovery. As the alcoholic/addict becomes successful in mastering these areas, you can expand the contract to cover other areas.

As a start, I advise my clients to start with four areas that should be obvious and natural skill sets in most people's recovery plans.

Fundamental areas of the recovery contract:

1. **Remain clean and sober**

   I recommend random drug testing at a center that has the proper equipment for testing and results. Please don't do this yourself. It could cause resentment between the two of you, and you should not be involved this personally in the recovery process. Anyway, the alcoholic/addict has to urinate in a cup and someone has to witness a clean specimen, and I don't think you want to participate in that. A word of warning: Professional drug testing at a local rehab facility is the litmus test whether the alcoholic/addict is really serious about their recovery. If they are, they will be only too happy to comply; if not, they will balk and list a dozen reasons or excuses why they can't do that. If they don't agree to the testing, all bets are off. It is not necessary to continue with the contract. They test outside the home, or there is no home to go to!

2. **Attend 12-step recovery meetings and/or see a professional substance abuse counselor**

   My recommendation is for them to attend at least three 12-step recovery meetings a week and initially to meet once a week with a counselor, then meet with a counselor every other week if recovery is going smoothly. Remember, the 12-step recovery meetings are for remaining clean and sober and working with others. Both the A.A. meetings and the counseling are for the emotional and psychological aspects of unloading the baggage from addiction as well as learning to live life on life's terms.

3. **Engage classes, employment, or volunteer work**

   Thirty to forty hours a week keeping busy and responsible is vital to the recovery plan. The person in recovery functions best when scheduled and accountable to others.

4. **Participate at home**

   It is important that they are expected to participate within the household, whether it's participation in chores, meals, activities, or whatever the family decides.

If any of the above (or others that you choose) are not met with the understanding that you both have already agreed to, be prepared to implement your consequences that were also in the contract. Obviously, there will be differences in the above depending on whether it is a child or a mate returning home. Redistribute accordingly.

If the alcoholic/addict is not going to have any involvement with friends or family and is planning to continue recovery on their own, or opt out of recovery altogether, then no recovery contract is needed. But keep in mind that even the slightest involvement from the family would be more likely to have a positive result if a written or strongly stated understanding is in place. For example, if their only involvement with the family is occasional meals, make sure it's clearly understood what time they are expected to be there and that you require a clean and sober dinner companion. Excessive tardiness or questionable sobriety should scratch the whole evening.

I can't stress enough or repeat myself enough that all the honest and accomplished work that has been done to get to this place of recovery needs the framework of an agreed-upon plan to keep all grounded and focused. Implementing consequences when the alcoholic/addict does not meet agreed upon goals or commitments is crucial to the plan's success.

Another important aspect of the recovery contract represents a potential routine for the alcoholic/addict and offers a tangible outline of behavior with achievable goals. They will come to respect and appreciate the rules and regulations of this agreement.

4-column recovery contract:

If you feel you need more of a visual contract, consider using a worksheet that breaks the main points into four columns.

- Column 1 will be for the goals and accomplishments that both you and the alcoholic/addict agree on and that you both feel are realistic. They should include both personal goals as well as recovery ones.

- Column 2 will address how the alcoholic/addict sees the

goal in column one playing out or coming to fruition. What footwork needs to be done to make this goal a reality?

- Column 3 is for a projected date for completion. As well, space should be available for either a check mark for completion or a new goal date if the projected date was not achieved.

- Column 4 will represent the consequences if the other columns have not been fulfilled.

The purpose of this contract being done together is that this way neither of you can say that you didn't understand what was said or what was expected. The alcoholic/addict must be an active participant in what can be accomplished in their treatment plan goals and its time line. Finally, they should understand and accept the consequences if those goals aren't adhered to or completed.

Most importantly, you *must* enforce them, or else don't bother having the plan at all. If your loved one is in an in-patient recovery program, such a contract might not take effect until they complete the program and return home or move into a sober living house where your involvement might be more integral than it was previously. Regardless, have a confirmed date soon after termination from their program is over for all to discuss and then implement the contract.

Recovery plan for Sharon's son

Let's say that the above plan is just too convoluted for you to implement. This was the case for my client Sharon, who felt that way regarding her own lack of stick-to-it-tiveness with her son who was coming out of a three-month residential rehabilitation program. Sharon tried to insist that her son go to a sober living house for six months instead of sharing an apartment with a buddy. He didn't agree to the sober living house. She wasn't happy about his decision, but she felt that she couldn't just abandon him and let him flounder financially.

Though this was not what I wished her to implement, I have learned over many years as a counselor that I can only push my clients so far to do what I think is the right and healthy thing when it comes to their involvement with their loved one, the alcoholic/addict. I would much prefer to go to a B plan or even a C plan than to let them have no helping hand at all.

Together we constructed a recovery plan:

- Sharon would pay for his first month's rent in full.

- Sharon would pay one-half of his second month's rent.

- Sharon would pay one-quarter of his third month's rent.

- Sharon's son would be available for random drug testing during this three-month period.

If at any time her son could not come up with the remainder of the rent past the first month, she would not augment the difference. If at any time her son tested positive, then the contract was null and void and her participation would only be to pay for her original intention of a sober living home and nothing else.

Sharon felt comfortable with this plan and confident that she could enforce it. This was the key for her, as it is important to remember that we all are different and our fiber for implementing the consequences varies from person to person. I instructed Sharon (as I do all my clients) to sleep on their decisions. What might empower them in my office may be more tempered when the dust settles.

I've had many clients wish to reward their loved one for clean and sober behavior. Frankly, I think that living a clean and sober lifestyle is reward itself, but let's look at some thoughts. Rewards seem to be more relevant to children and their substance-abuse issues than to adults. Parents often feel they need or want to reward their children for good behavior. I am all for rewarding honest, healthy actions, but as I said previously, the real reward should be a clean and sober lifestyle and all the riches that come with that.

Rewards

If you wish to reward your child with something tangible, let's look at a couple of options that may be fulfilling for both of you, and not just the carrot at the end of the stick for being a good boy or girl and doing the right thing.

One idea might be to plan a family vacation. Maybe pick somewhere that the recovering alcoholic/addict has never been and has always had a desire to visit. Depending on your finances and interest, anything from a camping trip to a Mediterranean cruise could be rewarding. While planning it together as a family, there is nothing wrong with discussing some fair boundaries and expectations that you all agree upon. These may have nothing to do with staying clean and sober but may fit in with the normal, everyday expectations of your family.

Some parents wish to purchase a car for their child or fund a number of months in an apartment as a way to demonstrate a vote of confidence in their child's budding sobriety. Again, these well-meaning parents might feel that a reward is definitely in order since their son or daughter has gone through such a difficult period in their life and has come out on the other side with flying colors. Some parents think that since children are frequently rewarded for good grades in school, why not reward them for getting clean and sober? This approach is not to my way of thinking.

However, if you are hell-bent on rewarding your child in a big way, please wait at least one year to eighteen months before you plunk down thousands of dollars for something. This way they can prove not only to you but also to themselves that they are responsible and dependable.

Truth be told, I'm leery about making a huge investment (i.e. a car) unless there is some fiscal responsibility held by the recovering alcoholic/addict. Discuss the idea with the recovering alcoholic/addict as to how they view their participation in the purchase. Maybe they will pay for one-half or one-third of the cost. This is a promising goal for the recovering alcoholic/addict to work toward, but accomplishing it may take a year or two. Maybe you could make an agreement with your child to pay for insurance, gas, and upkeep. The point is to hold them accountable not only to you but to themselves as well.

If they don't have the money for gas or insurance, then don't pay it for them in the hope that they'll pay you back. Parents have a way of forgetting or letting things slide to be the "good guys" so that their children will like them more or to help ease their difficulties. Don't forget to incorporate whatever ramifications both of you come up with if a car payment (or whatever is agreed upon) is not remitted on time. The recovering alcoholic/addict will function best when they know very clearly what the rules of the game are and what is expected of them.

Having your loved one in recovery invested in their own life gives them a sense of accomplishment and purpose. It can be a wonderful experience for everyone to share in the pride of ownership and participate in growth and development.

Your own recovery plan

Let's now turn our attention to your own personal recovery contract as it pertains to the alcoholic/addict in your life. If you can assemble our own guidelines and boundaries for yourself, then you will be prepared if your loved one doesn't hold up their end of the recovery bargain.

Our own recovery contract can implement rules and regulations that you have agreed upon with the alcoholic/addict, or it may pertain to plain life and have nothing to do with someone in recovery. I've come to accept and realize that we are all in some kind of recovery; maybe it's not mind-altering transformation, but it may be emotionally altering. So why not put together your own emotional or psychological recovery contract?

Using mantras in your 4-part personal recovery plan:

1. **Column one: "What do I want to see happen in my life?" and "What expectations am I seeking to accomplish?"**
   Usually it's a good idea to list two or three expectations. Whether I'm working on my relationships, hobbies, or finances, I include helpful mantras. My expectations usually include the following slogans: "Do the footwork and then let the game come to you" and "Turn my fear into faith."
   I am a very active person and thrive on being busy, busy, and

busy. Because I work hard on both my personal and professional life, I expect results. I was always told that if I work hard, then I will see results; but I have found that that's not necessarily true. So I have learned to stop expecting results (especially hard since I am a control freak) and do the footwork, step back, and let the game unfold as it may.

Though confident in many areas of my life, I can go into a tailspin if something doesn't work out the way I had hoped. I have been known to go into panic mode, especially financially, and I would spend days thinking that I need to sell my house. Ultimately, I worked things out without selling my house, but *yikes!*... how much time did I spend wringing my hands? "Turn my thoughts from fear to faith" has become a quiet, self-reflective discipline in my life. I like to remind myself that most all the fears from the past have never materialized, so I should understand that I'm right where I should be, experiencing whatever I should be at this moment.

2. **Column two: "How do I see my expectations of what I want to have happen performing their part in my becoming healthy?"**
As I write out how my expectations will lead to a fulfilling and healthy life, I keep reminding myself of mantras that have helped me in the past. "Hitting the pause button" when I find myself wanting to push the results faster than they may unfold is a good way to establish a more patient way for the future to unfold as it may. Also, focusing on something else that I wish to accomplish is a good way to take my mind off the narrow path of trying to control outcomes that, well, I just *can't* control.

In the last decade, I have become a very spiritual person. "Turning my will and care over to my Higher Power" helps to turn my malady of fear and worry into a strength of faith.

3. **Column three: "What is my time frame for change?"**
The time frame you put into this column is up to you. It can be at the end of a week, end of the month, or after several months. I like to take some time before turning the lights off on Sunday night to reflect on the week to see what kind of progress, if any, was made.

Instead of feeling like I'm not making progress, I remind myself to chart my progress "brick by brick." I see the image of me building my personal structure literally one brick at a time.

4. **Column four: "What are the consequences if the other columns are not adhered to?"**
    I'm certainly not going to punish myself for being more fearful than I would like or for being too controlling. No, I suggest that we do just the opposite of "lowering the boom." I remind myself to "be kinder and gentler." When a situation doesn't turn out quite how I had hoped it to, I breakdown where I went astray, what I might do a bit better next time around, and how I'd like to work toward that.

    I remind myself that "I will be taken care of" instead of punishing myself, since punishing only creates more worry and fear. I think if we are aware of our foibles and character defects and want to work on them a little bit at a time, even if it changes at the same pace as stalagmite growing, we are doing a heck of a good job.

Boundaries

Boundaries are a kissing cousins to our own recovery contract, but they can come in different shapes and forms more often and throughout the day. It can seem that we are always being tested by the alcoholic/addict. If our boundaries are not plastered to our brain and heart, then we can be caught off guard and stumble around in the dark. Keeping our boundaries very near and dear to us is important since it can be difficult to get back on track. We have to start over with our own credibility and be true certainly to ourselves but to others as well.

Boundaries are one of the most difficult things to implement and hold firm to when dealing with the alcoholic/addict in one's life. Whether upholding a curfew or expecting sobriety, our lives can often be fraught with a myriad of herky-jerky stops, and we end up with no consistent plan.

The alcoholic/addict has an uncanny way of manipulating us into trashing those boundaries as they hold the invisible weapons over our heads of baiting and punishing or bullying behavior. We can be paralyzed with fear of, "I'll show you. You'll be sorry for doing this!" We have been used to interpreting this as "I'm going to relapse, or worse yet kill myself, and it will be your fault."

Boundaries are scary because they hold an emotional line. If there is no follow through on ramifications, your intentions are quickly dismissed as frivolous, your credibility is shot, and your word is like quicksand.

Setting boundaries with children

As a counselor and parent, I am distressed when I hear the way some children talk to their parents. Yet I observe parents who rarely reprimanded their children for fear of reprisal or the withholding of love. Maybe children hear this way of interacting from other family members; they come to realize that since no action is taken, it must be an acceptable way to relate.

I am not denying that our children are the most important part of our lives, but it is vitally important that we don't forget about ourselves. Don't get sucked into something you are not comfortable with just to please others or because society says that this is what you are supposed to accept. Turn a deaf ear to those who judge your decisions but may never really know or have any knowledge or experience with a child with an addiction.

Sometimes boundaries are all we have to keep our dignity and self-respect alive. Though they are often painful to implement, it is worth the discomfort as the process invokes a feeling of self-empowerment and knowing that you are able to remove the tattoo that says "doormat" off your forehead.

Gretchen's boundary setting story

For a number of months, I worked with Gretchen—a caring, loving mother struggling with a daughter who had one foot in recovery and one foot out of recovery. Their connection was often brittle, but there were moments of bright sunshine and what seemed like a healthy balance of communication and respect between them.

However, her daughter became rude and indignant toward her. Gretchen feared that she was once again in her addiction. She was showing up late or not at all to family functions. When she did attend, she was disheveled, with dirty hair and clothes, and she made frequent trips to the bathroom. She was always ready for combat if anyone said anything she didn't like.

Through the roller coaster ride of her daughter's being in and out of recovery, Gretchen learned that any comment she made would fall on deaf ears and a steady stream of insults toward her was bound to flow like a fountain.

After weeks had passed since their last encounter, Gretchen's daughter contacted her as if nothing was wrong. She became incensed when her mother questioned her behavior the last time they were together, and she wouldn't just forget about it and move on.

Gretchen and I discussed her daughter's actions and what she felt her recourse should be. We determined that the best route was to respond in a neutral and loving way, yet I reiterated what her personal boundaries needed to be in order to have a relationship that was honest and respectful.

After hours of thought, Gretchen composed the following email. This might be difficult for some parents to read because they may think that no matter what their child does, a parent should always be accepting, regardless of the behavior or lack of respect shown.

Hi Brooke,

It has been a few days since you sent me a text, and I apologize for not responding sooner, but I wanted to get my thoughts in order. First and foremost, I love you.

You are my daughter and a day doesn't go by that I don't think of you and hope that you are well. It saddens me that our relationship isn't better and more on an even keel.

With that said, no matter whom I have a relationship with, respect, dignity and honesty comes with the territory.

For the past several months, I do not believe that you have shown me the respect, dignity and calm that I need/want, and these are important boundaries for me.

I don't want to list examples of where or why I have come to these conclusions as we both know what they are. I think you believe that just because I'm your mother I should accept you for who you are and how you act, and if I don't like your actions, I should just sweep my feelings under the rug and move on.

I accept you for who you are, but I am currently struggling with our relationship, which is void of everyday courtesy, kindness and dignity. It appears that whenever we discuss your actions (or try to) you defend, justify and punish me; rarely taking responsibility for them. The word "humble" or being genuinely sorry and making right by your mistakes doesn't seem to be part of your thinking.

My fear now is that if you have gotten this far in reading this, you may be saying, "I'm trying to reach out and all you are doing is slamming me . . . who needs this?" It is not my intention to thwart your intentions, but it is the healthy part of me that needs to start taking care of myself with stronger boundaries and clearer communication.

I am hopeful that one day you will say to me, "Hey, mom, my side of the street needs some massive cleaning, and I want to do anything I can to try and build a friendship with respect, dignity and love, not only because you're my mom, but probably a really good friend as well." That will be the day I will bring to the table the same thing and work hard to do my part and make our relationship the best it can be.

Love,
Mom

Though Gretchen was relieved to send this email, she was saddened as well. To this day, her daughter has never addressed her feelings.

Gretchen understands that until she is practicing a clean and sober lifestyle, she may not be capable. However, this correspondence emboldened Gretchen. She stated her boundaries and realized that she was ultimately taking care of herself in a healthy, nourishing way.

A Midwesterner's boundaries story

Let me give you another example of a combination of a personal recovery contract interlaced with boundaries. I worked with a woman from the Midwest who was struggling with her husband's alcoholic addiction. She has been married for over twenty-five years and truly loves her husband as best friend, lover, mate, and father to their two children. She told me she had been down the flimsy road of recovery with him several times before, but it has always been a hit-and-miss experience. She was exhausted and held her breath every time he walked through the door. She was always wondering whether he would be coming home from work clean and sober or three sheets to the wind.

She had tried threats, fights, sleeping in the other room, silence, non-participation in meals, separation at family time, and cancelling social events. She could bully her husband into recovery, but inevitably, anger, resentment, and a tense home life would prevail. Her husband talked about putting their life back on track, and he would embrace a recovery plan for a week or two. However, like clockwork, he would slowly slip back into his addiction. My client was exhausted and couldn't cope with another relapse, so together we crafted her own recovery contract/boundaries.

It was important that we segregated her desires that might have been spawned by anger versus those she was really capable of following through with. For example, her anger and frustration might have her threaten to file for divorce or leave in the middle of the night to an undisclosed place. These were knee-jerk reactions to his actions. Though we processed these by talking about the reality of such, we ultimately filed these away as an option if all others failed.

When her husband was clearheaded, my client calmly and with an even tone told him the details of her recovery contract for herself.

3-step personal contract:

1. If you decide to drink, then do not come home that night.

2. If you try to come home, the doors will be locked, the house will be dark, and I will move from our bedroom to another room.

3. The following day, I will leave the house for an extended stay and will not tell you where I am going, just that I need to get away.

- My client and I discussed where she could go—somewhere she could feel safe and comfortable.

- We discussed how long she would be gone and decided on one week.

- We composed a letter to leave on the table since she didn't want to have a face-to-face confrontation about her actions.

- She made a plan to keep a bag packed, keep her gas tank filled, and have her driving route planned out.

- She decided she could pull her car out of the driveway while her husband was at work.

- She told her children, now grown and living outside the home, of her plan and came up with a signal so she could communicate in the event of a real emergency.

When her husband broke their agreement about drinking, she followed through on her contract. When her husband got home and saw the note, he called her cell phone several times but to no avail. She did not answer his calls. In listening to his messages, they ranged from, "Who cares what you do. I'm glad you are gone"; and "You are the reason why I drink. You are insensitive and a terrible wife"; to "Please come back. I'll change . . . you'll see."

My client stayed away for the week like she had told him. Toward the end of that week, she called and left a message saying that they needed to talk about their future together and what it might look like, whether that meant a clean and sober partnership or them going their separate ways. My client was concerned that she might have to leave her home again. We decided that leaving was not going to be an option and that her husband would now be exiled from the residence.

She calmly stated that she would go on with life without him. After a few days of disgruntled behavior, which my client ignored (she also slept in a spare bedroom), he committed to really digging in and getting the recovery he needed. He didn't want to lose his wife and friend and knew that one more slipup would be the last. To the best of my knowledge, he is towing the line of sobriety and they are rebuilding a new relationship together. She is staying out of his recovery as it's none of her concern, but she is supportive and emotionally available to him while he navigates this difficult but oh so wonderful road to a new life.

Boundaries when grandchildren are involved

The examples go on and on. They come from all over the world and involve different issues and family members, but the hue and cry is always the same. Another client of mine, an elderly woman, was having difficulty with her alcoholic son. Every time they would spend time together, they would end up in an argument. He directed mean, cruel words toward her lack of mothering efforts and kindness for others.

Like many alcoholic/addicts, he threatened her with taking away something she loves and holds near and dear whenever she didn't comply with his demands. Her son is married with two beautiful children, and my client's grandchildren were his barter item. Her son intimidated my client to make her do what he wanted. If not, he would threaten her with "no time with your grandchildren." The dust would settle, and my client would sweep her disappointment and anxiety under the rug. She kept hoping that the next time they were together would be calmer and successful.

My client would go out of her way to make sure the visit was as good as it could be: the right food, a clean guest room, and anything else she could think of to keep the fur from flying. But no matter how painstakingly my client had planned for everything to be perfect, it of course wasn't. She was in a no-win situation, no matter what she did or said.

My client was supposed to head to California to watch the grand-children while her son and daughter-in-law were away on vacation. As planned, she went there a few days early, but this time she committed to laying out her plans to him for a comfortable visit. If her son didn't agree to her terms, she determined she would return home without having spent the special time with her grandchildren.

Sadly, an explosion between her and her son took place at every turn. My client had no choice but to leave with a heavy heart of disappointment and sadness. She had made her recovery contract/boundaries clear to him, and though she felt sad about her premature exit, both she and I were proud of her for following through on her words and intentions.

Taking back control

Some may feel that they are a failure if they abandon their relation-ship. Coming to this conclusion and realizing that the end is upon you can actually be incredibly empowering. Take some comfort in knowing that you have taken control of the situation. Sometimes it's the bravest option, because it requires you to face what you might think of as a failure, but is not. In life there really is no such thing as a crash-and-burn scenario. There are only lessons to be learned for a better, healthier go-around the next time.

Sometimes throwing in the towel is not just relegated to the alco-holic/addict but to the general public as well. Relationships can run their course whether they involve family, business associates, or friends. We need to make a change regardless of how painful or uncomfortable.

Joint custody—the empowerment of boundaries

What about boundaries between a divorced couple sharing custody? Many of my clients have come to me wondering how they should handle the relationship with their ex-spouse or significant other as it pertains to their children. Sadly, divorce or separation is common for alcoholics/addicts due to the presence of continued substance abuse or numerous unsuccessful attempts at sobriety.

I am not here to judge about the disposition of the marriage or partnership or to give comment as to whether the couple has done everything they can to save the relationship. Also, I am not a child psychologist, so options may be important to take into consideration other than my opinion on this issue.

However, if the die is cast, then so be it. However, the children involved are innocent to the situation and hopefully still have two parents who want to be participants in their lives. Rarely have I known a father or mother to abandon their children in order to live a life of substance abuse. I did have a client who shared that her ex-husband would rather live in a box, virtually homeless, and drink each day rather than have any contact with his children. This scenario makes for a heartbreaking state of affairs all around.

What are the options for the parent who has primary custody for the child/children while the other parent is trying to either work a clean and sober program or drink only on days when there's no involvement with the children? It goes without saying that all bets are off if one parent is totally irresponsible, has exhibited out-of-control behavior, or puts the children in danger.

A substantial amount of time must pass in order for the alcoholic/addict to demonstrate a responsible, tethered clean and sober lifestyle before supervised visits or co-parenting can occur.

Let's look at the circumstances in which the temperament of the alcoholic/addict parent does not present a risk to their child or children. The most important thing the custodial parent can do is to formulate a co-parental agreement. What I mean by this is that the primary custody parent should *write down* their expectations for when the child/children are in the supervision of the alcoholic/addict parent.

If the separation or divorce is somewhat amicable and the children's happiness and wellbeing is of paramount importance to both father and mother, then I have advised my clients to reiterate their hope and desire that the children can have two involved and loving parents.

A co-parenting agreement

The following letter is a short parental agreement based on the agreement a custodial client and I drafted together to present to his co-parenting partner.

> Dear Daniel,
>
> We have two wonderful children together, and they deserve both our love and attention as caring and responsible parents and adults; I know that you would not disagree.
>
> I am concerned about your alcohol intake. Though it is none of my business if you wish to drink or not, it is my concern if it happens while the children are in your custody. I'm certain we are both desirous of raising happy, healthy children, where we can both participate in their lives, so I propose the following:
>
> I will have the children three days a week unencumbered and you will have them three days a week. On the seventh day, we will use best efforts to share the company of our children jointly. In the event that is not possible for whatever reason, then the fourth day will rotate between us every other week.
>
> You will commit to picking up and returning the children on a certain day at a certain time, unless other arrangements have been made.
>
> You will not take the children outside an agreed upon mileage radius unless I approve beforehand.
>
> The children will call the custodial parent every night before bed, after school, or whatever time we firmly commit to.
>
> Neither one of us may make significant decisions regarding vacations, parties, medical issues, etc. without discussing and obtaining the approval of the other person prior to the intended date.

I need to hear from you by phone (not text or email) by 9:00 a.m. on the days that you have the children. Please be aware that if I don't, I will come and get them.

If I am not comfortable with your state of responsibility or I question your sobriety, I will contact child welfare services or get the police involved. As a concerned parent, I will do whatever the safest, healthiest, and most responsible steps are to ensure our children's best interest.

An agreement like this one may sound harsh to the alcoholic/addict, so be prepared for the possible backlash of anger and retaliation in some way. They may feel it is unfair to be on such a short leash, but as trust and dependability is restored, you can always extend the length of that leash.

If you feel so inclined, you may allow the alcoholic/addict parent to come up with their own proposal and possibly come to a mutual agreement and understanding. However, I caution you that staying clean and sober while in custody of the children should never be compromised. For example, a few social drinks at a family birthday party are not acceptable when the children are present or under the alcoholic/addict's supervision.

Regardless of how the contract shakes out between the two parents, the important factor here is that there is a solid commitment and understanding in writing. Bumping along the bottom and merely hoping things work out is a recipe for disaster. With a contract in place, neither party can say, "I thought that would be okay." Problems arise with verbal agreements that can be disputed by saying, "I didn't know that's what you wanted me to do." When it's in writing, confusion is less likely and, therefore, not knowing cannot be used as an excuse.

Our children are central to our lives, and their wellbeing should be a dominant part of our daily lives. A bit of uncertainty or uneasiness in putting together an agreement that can be clear, honest, and fair to both loving and caring parents is a small price to pay when it comes to establishing a safe, comfortable haven. A good agreement makes for a safe situation in which each parent can enjoy their time with their children yet not worry when the children are with the other parent.

Special occasions

The last boundary I want to share is about those fantasy holidays that everyone hopes to re-create that Norman Rockwell painting depicting the perfect family meal and celebration. Special occasions are a lovely thought, and for some the preparation and anticipation for holidays such as Thanksgiving, Christmas, Hanukah, and birthdays is joyous and an opportunity to be and feel festive. Family and friends come together to celebrate taking out the old and bringing in the new.

But what if there is an alcoholic/addict in your life? You both may desire to spend all or part of the celebration days together, yet you may both feel anxious nonetheless. Though you might nervously anticipate problems, please don't bring up old examples of how the alcoholic/addict let you down in the past. Doing so might provoke an argument that serves no purpose. The desire to have the family together can be a strong pull for any parent, spouse, sibling, or friend. Even with the hopes, desires, and promises that everything will go as planned, it is that wise parent, spouse, sibling, or friend who presents a clear head as to how they would like to see the festivities gel when it comes to the involvement of their loved one, the alcoholic/addict.

For healthy openers, you will be more comfortable and confident if you keep in mind that *you* are in control, not the alcoholic/addict. Taking an active role establishes fair yet concrete boundaries and keeps your expectations to a minimum.

Concepts that make the difference between a successful occasion and a disastrous one:

1. **Deliver your boundaries and expectations in a timely manner**
    Discuss these boundaries at least one week before the holiday activity will take place.

    For example: "I need you to get in the right frame of mind for the party next week. I need to know you understand and agree to my boundaries."

2. **Carefully choose your boundaries**

   Pick boundaries that are important to you and *must* be adhered to by the alcoholic/addict; if they do not agree, then they will not be welcomed to participate in the family festivities.

   For example: "I expect you to arrive sober, at the designated time, well groomed, and dressed appropriately."

3. **Establish concise boundary statements**

   Keep these boundary statements simple, doable, and to the point.

   For example: "I expect you to be here at five o'clock; if you're going to be even one minute late, then I expect you to call me and give me an update on your estimated arrival time."

4. **Clearly define your expectations and consequences**

   Make your expectations and the consequences clear. If they live with you, make it clear that you will ask them to stay away until the event is over if you smell alcohol on their breath or they act intoxicated or high.

   For example: "If I smell alcohol on your breath when you arrive, I will not let you in."

5. **Be firm when stating your boundaries, expectations, and consequences**

   Don't defend yourself regarding your decisions. If you don't engage and you stay neutral, you will be perceived as having self-respect and a plan that is well thought out.

   For example: "I would like you to join us, but you're only invited if you understand and agree to the boundaries I'll be enforcing."

6. **Set clear consequences that both parties understand**

   Have clear ramifications if your conditions are not met. IMPORTANT: Make sure that you both understand what those consequences are so no one can dispute a misunderstanding or feign ignorance as to the intention of the plan.

   For example: "I've written down everything we've talked about so we have a clear understanding. Do you have any questions or concerns?"

If they don't like your holiday rules and regulations, be committed to a response like, "It makes me sad that you won't be joining us, but that's your choice." They now have to shoulder all the responsibility for their decision even though they may try to blame you.

Don't let your boundaries be built on quicksand. Don't acquiesce because the alcoholic/addict spins an excuse as to why they have not lived up to their end of the bargain. If you begin to waver, they are likely to resort to tugging at your heartstrings or to yelling and screaming when they don't get their way.

Please don't fall prey to thinking, "I'll overlook this because it's the holidays." Be cautious to not relax your boundaries by thinking, "It's the holidays, and I just don't want to be unhappy or make my loved one unhappy." Letting the boundaries lax will make for a lose-lose scenario all around.

In addition, please don't let a family member rope you into accepting the alcoholic/addict on whatever terms they wish, using the excuse that they haven't seen him or her for a long time and it would make them happy to connect up with them again. Instead, make it clear that they are certainly welcome to get together before or after the event or on another day. Let them know if you need them to meet at a designated spot away from the home or celebration venue.

Tell the other family members what that arrangement is so everyone is on the same page and there can be no surprises. Do keep an open mind that if the alcoholic/addict or any of your family members decides to opt out of the family festivities for one reason or another (not comfortable with your rules, doesn't care for someone who is going to be there, isn't ready for a public appearance), then respect that with no guilt, judgment, or cajoling placed upon them.

Expectations

Finally, let's look at expectations. We all have them. They are really what keep our hopes and dreams alive. Expectations can be healthy and keep us open and moving forward, but they can be harmful if they are not realistic and cannot meet our specifications. Unrealistic expectations can ruin our mood and, in turn, ruin a special day.

3 thoughts to keep in mind as a training ground:

1. Keep your expectations in check. Realize that you are dealing with someone who might not be as true to their word as you would like them to be. Though you might be disappointed, you won't be surprised.

2. Try not to involve the family too much. You may have a jubilant desire that the whole family will be together for some occasion, but this desire can lead to disappointment. Conversely, help your family to keep their expectations curbed as well.

3. If your expectations are not met, please remember this is not an affront to you. It's not personal; it's just the nature of their disease and what they may be struggling with at this particular time.

Boundaries and expectations are extremely hard to implement and to curb. I know this all too well as I have struggled with them for the last twenty years while dealing with my own family's substance abuse issues. If you follow your plan, you can swim away from any event successfully.

Julian's holiday expectations

A few years ago my client Julian was going to be spending his first holiday with his sometimes actively addicted, sometimes recovering daughter. He didn't know whether his daughter would show up with her sweatshirt hood pulled so low she could barely see her chin or with clean hair, make-up, and a smile on her face. Julian stated his boundaries with gentle but firm communication, and his daughter agreed to abide by them.

Julian prayed to God that his daughter would be obliging, as it would have broken his heart if he had to turn her away. We talked it over, and Julian was prepared to turn her away if he felt compromised or disrespected. Julian was in the frame of mind that it was going to be an enjoyable evening. He was committed to being true to her boundaries and to leaving his expectations in the trunk of the car.

As it turned out it was a 50/50 compromise. Though his daughter's appearance wasn't what Julian would have liked to see, his daughter was pleasant, on time, and communicative. Julian didn't examine her too closely to see if she was high or not, as he honestly didn't want to know as long as his daughter was respectful. Julian's time with his daughter was so uncertain—so sketchy with her mood swings, irresponsibility, and rampant addiction—that Julian felt content with the bird in the hand. He reported back to me that he felt grateful that on that occasion all was pretty okay with his little family world.

Focus on a positive outcome

Sometimes expectations need to be a bit flexible. As the one implementing these expectations, you need to pick your battles. What's a deal breaker, and what can you live with for a few hours? If things get rough or out of control, you can always thank everyone for a good time and go home early. Maybe all your loved one can handle is a few hours of being "good." So take those moments, enjoy them as a Kodak moment, and leave with a pretty good taste in your mouth.

Please remember that you too deserve an enjoyable encounter with your loved one. Whether it is a holiday dinner, camping trip, or coffee and conversation, don't allow your loved one, who may still be struggling in various parts of their disease, to take that away from you. If you don't spend this specific arranged time, there will be other opportunities.

Recovery contracts, boundaries, and healthy expectations are all we have to keep our dignity and self-respect alive. Though they are often painful to implement, it is worth the discomfort as the process invokes a feeling of self-empowerment and knowing that you are able to peel the tattoo of "doormat" off your forehead.

Processing Questionnaire

Processing questionnaire for the recovery contract:

- Who is the alcoholic/addict for whom you are implementing this recovery contract?

- What are the goals?

- How are they going to see them accomplished?

- What is the time frame?

- What are the consequences?

Processing questionnaire for boundaries:

- To whom do you wish to implement boundaries around?

- What are some of those boundaries?

- Are you comfortable with them and find them doable so as not to falter if challenged?

- Are you willing to terminate the relationship (even for only a bit of time) if that person doesn't respect your boundaries?

Processing questionnaire for expectations:

- Are your expectations geared toward a specific person?

- What are those expectations?

- Are they realistic?

- What are your expectations for yourself?

- Are they realistic?

- What is your plan if those expectations fall short from either the other person or you?

CHAPTER 7

WHY IS BEING AN ENABLER TO THE ALCOHOLIC/ADDICT SO DETRIMENTAL?

In my many years of being a family substance abuse counselor as well as dealing with my own family's addiction issues, I've come to know that the most detrimental and hazardous aspect in the world of addiction and recovery is the enabling and rescuing of one for the other. Enabling another person is telling them that *they* can't do whatever task or challenge is put before them, therefore, *you* need to do it for them. You are cutting them off at the knees with the interference and by not allowing them the grace to succeed or the ability to learn a potentially valuable life lesson.

Enabling an alcoholic/addict can be the most destructive and manipulative action one can take. The result of that enabling can sever family relationships, create havoc, and add damage to an already volatile situation. One of the most painful casualties of war is when outsiders (other family members, close friends) try to play hero and step in. Outside involvement can derail the boundary work that the immediate family has taken loads of time through trial and error to incorporate into life with their loved one. In a few moments, the good foundation you've been building can be blown to smithereens.

Relatives who rescue and enable

One of my clients was trying desperately to help her daughter in recovery. When the going got rough between them and she wanted things her way—not the healthy way—my client's sister would swoop into the picture without any conference. Her sister had zero experience with addiction. She had never even stepped into an Al-Anon or open A.A. meeting. In addition, she had never had children nor did she understand her niece's issues. Then she went on to blame her sister for her niece's unbalanced upbringing. Without any professional guidance or counseling, the aunt would pick up the reins and give her niece money or use her connections to find her a job. The aunt allowed the alcoholic/addict to treat her with as much disrespect as the young woman wanted to from day to day—and it was all okay.

People who stick their noses into other people's lives are playing emotional, psychological, and sometimes even physical Russian roulette with the alcoholic/addict—whether in recovery or not. The only job of those outside the alcoholic/addict's primary circle is to encourage success. This role happens off the playing field, where the loved ones observe and cheer unobtrusively from the grandstand.

The rescuer/enabler

What does the "rescuer" or "enabler" look like? Why are these labels so common to so many well-meaning family members and friends whose lives are entangled with the alcoholic/addict?

As caring, compassionate people, we naturally and instinctively want to protect and help our loved ones. There is a universal drive in both animals and human beings that beckons us to stand between what we see as a potentially harmful situation and the ones we love, especially if those loved ones are weak or sick.

Enabling and rescuing someone who is an alcoholic/addict can range from lying and covering up the infractions from their intoxication to throwing what you think is a lifeline. Yet that intentional helping hand could result in a dangerous outcome. You probably have no idea what their patterns or habits are regarding their addiction. Innocently, your enabling or rescuing could unintentionally continue to promote the out-of-control and dangerous behavior.

There is a fine line between being part of the solution and being part of the problem. The challenge comes in breaking the habit of being part of the problem, and becoming part of the solution instead. Why is this so hard to do when we know that rescuing our loved one (the alcoholic/addict) is truly detrimental not only to their wellbeing but to ours also?

19 reasons why the call to rescue or enable is so hard to shut out:

1. We like to feel wanted and needed. It is a momentary adrenaline rush when for a brief instant we are the center of someone else's world. They thank us and are so grateful for our help since chances are that someone else has said no to them. You are their hero *du jour* . . . and that is a heck of a warm and fuzzy feeling. The addiction (yes, I said addiction) of enabling and rescuing others (a family member or the mailman) over and over again is usually found holed up somewhere in the psyche of people who might not have enough going on in their own personal life, or what they have is not as fulfilling as it should be.

2. We are bored and, therefore, ripe for wearing the enabling and rescuing crown. If you're bored, it's easy to shelve that boredom by foisting your opinion or even trying hard to take over another's life when you don't feel that they are doing a good enough job on their own or you don't approve of their lifestyle.

3. We are feeling insecure or uncomfortable in our own skin, so we seek attention from others to satisfy these needs. A wonderful way to fill that void is to enable and rescue someone you think is screaming out for a life preserver. Whether they are or not, you think you know best. By donning the hero's rescue cape, your hope is that not only will you be praised for your efforts, insights, and sensitivity but also you will take a well-deserved bow because of your sixth sense.

4. We hope against all hope that tomorrow will be different. We buy into thinking that something has changed, We want to believe there's hope for an honest stab at rehab, even though the other attempts have unfortunately derailed. Or we figure if we do this deed this one more time, everything will improve.

We promise ourselves, or even tell the alcoholic/addict, that this is the last time we are going to do or will ever need to do whatever it is they want.

5. We like to be the ones who "saved the day." The pleasure we get from rescuing the alcoholic/addict feels good, but there's excess ego in a person who creates and then enjoys their own standing ovation. Some people boast while others sheepishly agree that their intervention of help is what has truly turned the corner for this person. True virtue and philanthropic activity, no matter how big or small, is only healthy and pure if one doesn't toot their horn over their own grand gestures. We need to find pleasure from within rather than from rescuing to receive accolades from others.

6. We want to be liked, which is our ego getting in the way again. More true for parents than for a spouse, rescuers want to be pals with the alcoholic/addict. Sometimes parents blame themselves and want to make up for being absent or unavailable to their children during critical times in life. Thinking "better late than never," they want to wipe out the past, hoping they will be able to thwart off the bad stuff and have a relationship that is now better than before. The parent may think they are earning brownie points for being a good chum; but trust me, the good deed is short lived in the eyes of the alcoholic/addict. Your chummy relationship only lasts until the next request, which can be just a few hours away.

7. We believe the alcoholic/addict is too frail, challenged, or damaged to help themselves. I have heard from so many clients that their child is bipolar, depressed, or traumatized. Non-enabling or non-rescuing is even more important than ever when it comes to an alcoholic/addict who had a traumatic experience growing up. Sure, you can offer them some professional help to overcome their issues that might be holding them back from getting on with life on life's terms, but don't let these maladies be used as a get-out-of-jail card or allow the alcoholic/addict to continue their irresponsible or out-of-control behavior.

8. We feel competitive, so we feel like we are winning when we rescue the "weaker" alcoholic/addict. Outsiders may enjoy throwing the parent or spouse of the alcoholic/addict "under the bus" if they are jealous of them. Rescuing is a way to outshine them. Competition between siblings in particular can rear its ugly head if given a chance. It can be a perfect time for one sibling to say, "I never did think they had it together. See what's happened? I was right all the time."

9. We are afraid that saying no to the alcoholic/addict could lead to their suicide. What if a loved one dies because we didn't do what they asked of us? What if we could have stopped it? This is the fear of many parents when they want to say no to a child who asks them to do this or do that. When they leave the house and slam the door, it's difficult not to run after them and say okay. Rather than saying no, we agree to them doing this or that, along with the admonishment to "just be careful" or to be home at a certain hour. Please, please don't fall for this. You cannot keep a short leash on your loved one at all times. If they plan on stepping in front of a train, then sadly that is their decision. No matter what you do or say, you have no control over them. With that said, usually the alcoholic/addict has no intention of taking their life; most times, they just want what they want when they want it. This is a grown-up temper tantrum that they use now that they are too big to lie down on the floor and stamp their feet. Having said that, if you feel there is a true possibility of a suicide attempt, then seek help immediately.

10. We see them as sick and not responsible for their actions. Much like seeing the alcoholic as damaged (number 7), we see the alcoholic/addict as a victim. When we enable folks, we justify their actions by saying that the alcoholic/addict has a disease and is not responsible for their actions. We make excuses about why they've been fired from their job or dumped by their girlfriend/boyfriend. We tell ourselves that the situation that is out of their control and that they can't help but to act this way.

11. We're not ones to hurt others feelings, and saying no will hurt their feelings. No is a one-word sentence that is very hard for many folks to say. It usually is accompanied with a justification for their answer. Yet if we have the fortitude to express what we're really feeling, then we could just say no, followed by "What part of no don't you understand?" Being polite and kind may be much more important to those who can't utter the two-letter answer. We need to learn that it's okay to turn someone down and not be afraid we will end up on their poop list.

12. We feel afraid of the alcoholic/addict's anger, punishment, or retribution. I remember that when I stopped enabling my alcoholic husband, he would lash out with his anger and hurtful comments. He would also threaten to tell the world what a horrible counselor or friend or wife or mother I was. Until I could muster up the strength to say, "Fine, go ahead," I would backpedal and make nice. I didn't feel I had the strength to put out the too many fires that were in front of me.

13. We are afraid the alcoholic/addict may do something "bad" (act out) and then blame us for their actions. You probably know the "I'll show you or you'll be sorry" attitude. Unlike threatening to kill themselves, this hue and cry is very commonly connected with the blaming statement, "You're the reason I relapsed," or "You're to blame that I am the way I am." Their attitude of feeling sorry for themselves goes along with their blaming refrains.

14. We feel afraid for ourselves and what will become of us. Being choked with fear has many people doing things that they later regret. Fear is a powerful state of mind. Fear can blind us, and it can lead us to hitting the pause button and stepping back to reevaluate the problem. We are often afraid of the alcoholic/addict in our life because we just don't know what's coming next. Not rocking the boat stems from fear. We fear the outcome of not acquiescing is just too great on us emotionally, physically, or financially. So we prefer to keep the peace. However, we are letting ourselves be held hostage by the alcoholic/addict—by their feelings and actions, but essentially by our own fear.

15. We care about how others perceive us. We think we will be perceived poorly or as not caring about our family members or friends if we don't rescue the alcoholic/addict. Some friends and family members have short or selective memories. They conveniently forget about all the attempts to help our loved one overcome and get help with their addiction. When we finally hit our bottom and say, "Enough is enough! I don't have any more strength or energy to go through this yet again," then we are judged as not caring. How can that be true when we've continually done so much?

    I once ran into a family member and got to talking about my daughter's relapse yet again. I explained that I just couldn't roll up my sleeves as it was too painful and emotional for me. I explained that all I could offer were prayers at night that she would find her way. He said that he would never give up on his daughter and would do whatever it took to help her. His wife said, "Sure, that's easy to say now, but you are not faced with that issue."

    Who knows what you would do if and when you're faced with continued relapses. No one wants to be perceived as an uncaring or "bad" parent. When it comes to people who judge from a place where they have no idea what life is like for you and the alcoholic/addict in your life, my advice is that if you have to cut ties with these people for your own wellbeing, then so be it.

16. We've become too weary, too lazy, or too frightened to implement change. Being down the road of addiction and recovery can be very draining and will suck a lot of the life out of you. After a while, we just can't do the boundary dance anymore, so we turn a deaf ear to them and allow the alcoholic/addict to do what they want, when they want.

17. This "dance" has been part of our lives for so long that we don't know what purpose we would have without it. Many people find an odd kind of solace in wringing their hands over the actions of the alcoholic/addict in their life. We want to do something about it, but our actions are nonexistent. I have often mentioned to my clients when I find that we have gone over the same territory again and again that maybe this is what keeps them functioning.

Maybe they think their life would feel empty or unfulfilled if they didn't have their loved one's disposition to worry about.

18. We feel a need to protect family members from embarrassment, scorn, or ridicule. This is attached to security fears. The fear is that if the addiction issues get out into the community, then a negative domino effect might ensue. This is a common fear when the alcoholic/addict is the breadwinner, but this fear is in operation whenever the addiction issues might negatively impact the family, especially the children.

   Many family members don't want to rock the boat or highlight their life problems, so they ignore the situation, turn a deaf ear, or bury themselves in their own world. If somehow the addiction monster happens to stray from its cave, it's an easy coverup to say that the alcoholic/addict is getting help, or doing much better. Anything is better than saying, "Yes, life is difficult now, and we as a family unit are struggling with addiction issues." Wouldn't that be a courageous thing to say? There is a certain respect given to someone who steps up to the plate like that and opens the door for others to be open and honest.

19. We need to protect ourselves from embarrassment, scorn, or ridicule. It is human nature to wonder what happened in a family unit when you hear about addiction issues. Many family members won't or don't go to Al-Anon, Alcoholics Anonymous meetings, or a counselor. They don't want anyone in the community to know of their "problem" or what goes on behind closed doors. One client's mother would say to her daughter, "We peel our own potatoes."

We all fall into some of these categories at times, whether these issues revolve around the alcoholic/addict or not. Hopefully, we fall out of these categories again, depending on the situation. It takes strength, confidence, and fortitude to resist the temptation to enable and rescue. But it's worth the effort, for it will produce a healthier lifestyle for not only the alcoholic/addict but also for you.

Rescuing or helping?

So what is the difference between rescuing and helping? As difficult as some situations may be to witness—incarcerated for a DUI, fired from a job—events pertaining to our loved ones' actions need to unfold as they are meant to, not how we want them to. If enabled or rescued, the person struggling with addiction is prevented from experiencing the repercussions of their decisions or the consequences that are derived from irresponsible or out-of-control behavior.

Sloane's story

A good, healthy example of someone helping and not rescuing is my client Sloane. Sloane was married to an alcoholic who bounced between living a clean and sober lifestyle and relapsing. Soon after their marriage, Sloane's husband became quick to anger and was easily provoked. Their relationship developed a very poor, walking-on-eggshells form of communication.

Sloane never stopped loving her husband, but she had come to the end of her rope in the relationship. She couldn't live with his instability or impatience anymore. They had been married only a few years and had no children, so Sloane requested a separation. After another relapse, he came to admit that he had hit his bottom. After a week clean and sober, he called Sloane and asked for yet another chance. He wanted to try and salvage the relationship as well as save himself from himself. He realized many of the things that had gone wrong during the marriage and his relapses (Sloane had lost count by now). He opened his eyes to what he needed to do to put the pieces of his life back together.

He felt that if he had the goal of rebuilding himself as well as their relationship, then he might be able to really commit to a clean and sober lifestyle. Sloane reiterated that she did not want to continue a relationship with him at this time; however, she told him that maybe sometime in the future they might. There had been some emotional and financial wreckage that had accompanied his last relapse. It would have been easy for Sloane to write a check for the financial problems and to provide transportation and even housing to support and encourage her husband toward sobriety, and not expect anything in return. Yet she knew that would be rescuing and not helping.

Instead, she proposed her participation as more of a friend. She began to listen with empathy, gently offering advice if asked while encouraging his goals and dreams and presenting personal, healthy objectives for the two of them to strive toward. They began rebuilding their emotional relationship slowly as well as implementing new plans and objectives for payment plans and other specifics.

Sloane felt confident she was helping in a loving way while staying grounded in strong boundaries and guidelines. Sloane's husband appreciated her fortitude and was grateful for her help. In reality, he didn't want to be rescued; he preferred picking himself up by his own bootstraps. He could prove to Sloane and himself the commitment he had to his recovery. He knew that working hard to rebuild his life his way would mean more in the long run and, hopefully, stave off the relapse itch.

Questions to ask yourself

If you are coming up with answers that include bailing out your loved one with cash or shouldering some of their legal ramifications, then your crown of rescuing is polished to a blinding glow that's just not healthy for either of you. If you are standing back and allowing incidents to play out as they may, yet presenting emotional and specific guidelines of support, then the report card for help will be A+. To assess yourself as to whether you are supporting or enabling your loved one, be truthful with yourself periodically in asking two simple questions:

"Am I helping or rescuing?"
"Am I enabling or keeping my distance?"

Processing Questionnaire

If the enabler is someone other than you:

- Who is being enabled?

- Who is doing the enabling?

- In what ways is the enabler promoting the out-of-control and dangerous behavior?

- What is your plan for helping the enabler to take a step back from rescuing the alcoholic/addict?

If the enabler is you:

- When have you been an enabler?

- Why did you do it, or why are you still doing it?

- What was the outcome, or what do you hope the outcome will be?

- Why do think this person you are enabling isn't capable of figuring it out by themselves?

- How can you step back from enabling this person?

- How can you exchange your views that promote enabling for ones that offer support without interference?

CHAPTER 8

WHY IS IT DIFFICULT TO COMMUNICATE WITH THE ALCOHOLIC/ADDICT?

Communication is an art all to itself. Whether it comes trippingly off the tongue, through expressive eyes, facial inflections, foot tapping, moans, groans, or whatever body language we are transmitting, it's all some type of communication.

In an instant, we hear or see what that person is saying to us and react accordingly. Most of the time we are prepared with what's coming; consequently, we engage accordingly. But it's a whole new verbal ball game when we communicate (or try to) with the alcoholic/addict.

Baiting and punishing

Let's look at some common banter your loved one might try to rope you into in order to engage you in a senseless round of dialogue. The alcoholic/addict doesn't see this as anything other than keeping you an active participant in their life, regardless of whether you have covered the same ground over and over. After a while you are exhausted and have grown weary of answering the same questions and concerns repeatedly with nothing being resolved.

This is what I call baiting and punishing. First, you are led to defending yourself; second, while doing so, you end up engaging in a pointless and fruitless heated discussion. Baiting and punishing is threatening the family or friend with loaded questions in which the alcoholic/addict wants you to respond a certain way by meeting their demands either physically or verbally.

The following comments are perfect examples that seem to come up like clockwork when the alcoholic/addict is angry, bored, restless, or lonely. Maybe they are looking for a reason to relapse, and any one of these statements if not answered to their specs will be the ticket they are looking for. Please know that no matter how you respond, your response is likely to be wrong since there is little or no sensibility in communicating with them.

Baiting and punishing statements:

- "I'm always letting you down."

- "I guess I'm just a bad person."

- "If you cared about me, you would do this for me."

- "I can't do anything right."

- "You've always liked my sister (or brother) better than me."

- "You just want me to leave."

- "I don't know why you don't trust me."

- "I guess this is what you want, right?"

- "You have no respect for me."

- "I don't make enough money for you. You really should be with someone who has an endless cash flow."

- "I'm not as smart as you; that's why you know all the answers."

- "You just don't love me anymore."

The family member or friend is usually trapped into defending and justifying with responses to the baiting and punishing statements.

Defending and justifying responses:

- "Of course not."

- "Don't be silly."

- "That's not true."

- "Okay, what would you like me to do to show you that you're wrong?"

- "No, let me explain."

- "You're wrong. That's not what I was thinking."

- "Why would you say that?"

Remember that the alcoholic/addict isn't really looking for the answer. Even if you give them a loving, thoughtful response, it will most likely appease them only for a short time.

After the weariness of going over this same diatribe for months, possibly years, and getting nowhere, you'll understand the need for redirecting this routine by responding differently. Try hard not to respond with a question. Questions can be loaded with potential conflict. In addition, asking questions allows the alcoholic/addict to control their response and gives them a sense of power, for you are held captive in waiting for their reply.

The objective now is to redirect your response with the following words or something similar. Don't respond with a question such as, "Why do you feel that way?" for that is an open invitation for engagement and possible conflict.

Statements to stop baiting and punishing:

- "I'm sorry you feel that way."

- "I didn't say that."

- "I think you may have misheard me."

- "Please don't put words in my mouth."

- "This must be difficult for you."

- "I'm sorry you're sad (or unhappy, or lonely or frustrated)."

- "That just won't work for me."

- "It is not healthy for me to participate in this with you."

- "I have answered this before and my answer now isn't any different."

Another simple solution is simply to walk away calmly, without any discussion or anger. Don't invoke your own punishing intentions. If you don't take the bait, the alcoholic/addict has nowhere to go.

We all have buttons that when pushed cause us to react with a less-than-favorable or less-than-mature response. If the alcoholic/addict is an intimate part of your life, they will know what sets you off and what an especially sensitive issue is for you.

If you once confessed to the alcoholic/addict that you felt you were not a particularly good parent, don't allow them to have a field day during an argument by bringing up your parenting inadequacies as proof that you're also not a good mate or good friend to others. This is a good example of baiting. Be careful of the hook. Be mindful of when it's coming. Prepare a plan to swim away successfully and unscathed.

Staying neutral

Why are staying neutral and not engaging so important in our communication with the alcoholic/addict? A car that is in neutral doesn't go anywhere—neither forward nor backward.

Staying neutral with the alcoholic/addict means you have no opinion one way or the other. Neutral means finding that middle ground where you are neither validating nor challenging what the alcoholic/

addict is communicating to you.

Staying neutral is safe. No one can come back and blame you for saying this or that, encouraging this action or that behavior. When you stay neutral, you turn the decision over to the alcoholic/addict for them to make on their own. You are empowering them with their own choice, and at the same time you are empowering yourself with a commitment to neutrality. The alcoholic/addict will be afforded the opportunity to learn from their decision, not yours. That decision will either garner positive results or not, but either way they will be in charge of that, not you.

Staying neutral cannot be totally effective without not engaging. If you can be successful in implementing both of these concepts, then I promise you will feel more grounded and confident, with renewed self-respect and dignity about your interchange. Your relationship with the alcoholic/addict will take on a new dimension because you have started to "short circuit" their thinking by responding differently than you have on previous occasions.

Sometimes it's difficult to stay neutral when you feel that your loved one really wants your opinion, insight, or help. I have compiled some neutral and safe retorts for you to consider when they are genuinely seeking your guidance.

8 neutral and safe retorts:

1. "You've asked for my opinion, but it may not be what you want to hear."

2. "I don't know enough about the situation or have enough facts to make a comfortable assessment."

3. "Use your own best judgment."

4. "I think I'm too close to the situation for an unbiased opinion."

5. "You seem to have given this enough thought to make a decision."

6. "I really have no opinion one way or the other."

7. "I'm uncomfortable getting in the middle of this."

8. "I've addressed this issue before, so you know how I feel."

Remember that the words that come out of your mouth need to be neutral. Your tone, attitude, and expressions need to follow suit. If you say, "Use your own best judgment," but your inflection is conveying, "You really are an idiot," or "That's the dumbest thing I've ever heard," then you become ineffective because your attitude will trump your words.

Hitting the pause button

Working hand in hand with staying neutral is the ability to take a breath, hit the pause button, and "think twice/act once." Those few precious seconds in which you breathe and hit the pause button might allow you to think twice and act once. It will give you time to regroup and respond with clear thought rather than reaction or emotion. Probably after years of manipulative conversations and actions, the alcoholic/addict knows what kind of response they will evoke. If you pause, stay neutral, and do not engage, then you can put yourself in control. Do not hand the baton over to the alcoholic/addict to conduct the exchange.

All of us have knee-jerk reactions to the things that can push our buttons. Some of us can go from 0 to 60 faster than others. Many of us feel that if we don't retaliate immediately, either with words or actions, then it is a sign of weakness. Getting angry too often can be like crying wolf. No one will believe that you are justified in your anger if you do it too frequently. Hence, hitting the pause button allows you to take stock of the situation before acting on it impetuously. This gives you time to calculate your next action so you can be coming from a place of confidence and stability rather than emotion and passion. It also demonstrates restraint and maturity. It will signify to the alcoholic/addict (sometimes more aptly described as the "bully") that they do not have the power to "get your goat."

The silence that you maintain can be unnerving and uncomfortable to the person struggling with addiction. They are not used to this kind of response and may feel anxious about what's coming next. Changing the routine from what it once was will show that you are starting to map out your own attitude and communication. Therefore, they will see that you are becoming more resilient to their behavior.

Though these concepts are simple on the surface, they can be challenging to incorporate. We are easily distracted by wanting to protect our loved one from making bad decisions or using poor judgment. We feel we know better and most likely do, but we cannot beg, cry, manipulate, or force another person see things our way if they don't want to. If you do nothing else but hit the pause button, you are giving yourself a chance to curb your anger or frustration. During this time, you can find those neutral words you need to form your answer.

The passive-aggressive alcoholic/addict

As I previously mentioned, communicating with the alcoholic/addict is a difficult thing and a creative challenge. Obviously, there can be little or no communication if the alcoholic/addict is so entangled in their addiction that they can barely string two sentences together. If the alcoholic/addict is in an addictive state, then communication is worthless and one should not waste their energy. They will only hear what they want, ignore you altogether, walk away, or veg out.

Often the alcoholic/addict might be working a clean and sober program but hasn't dealt with the other issues that come with the new lifestyle. Someone who is working a clean and sober program but is still angry and resentful is substantially more frustrating to communicate with than the zoned-out addict.

3 stages of passive-aggressive communication with the alcoholic/addict:

1. The alcoholic/addict wants something you have. They set the stage for what they want by starting out very nice, almost sugary sweet.

2. You respond because you are feeling generous, even though you know in your heart and from past experience that you shouldn't be engaging with this person since the outcome has always been so unsatisfactory.

3. All of a sudden, the dialogue is going way off course from the initial intent. Good intentions and communications are out the window as the initial passivity of the alcoholic/addict (Dr. Jekyll) has now turned into the aggressive person (Mr. Hyde).

Sherrie's email exchange

My client Sherrie shared with me a passive-aggressive interchange (via email) that she had with her ex-husband. They had had little or no communication since their divorce, so this email came out of left field. After all the back-and-forth communication was over, and she was exhausted trying to decipher what he wanted or didn't want, Sherrie was reminded that this was one of the many reasons why she was no longer married to him.

They had rescued a young dog named Arnie from the Humane Society. He is now much older, and Sherrie has custody.

Blake: How is Arnie? I miss him very much.

Sherrie: Arnie is fine and in good health. However, I don't know how long that will be. If you want to visit him, just let me know when so I can make arrangements.

Blake: First, it is comforting to know Arnie is fine, healthy, and I'm sure, happy. Second, thank you for your offer; it is very kind. However, I believe the "devil is in the details." I'm not sure what "arrangements" can be made, what form or shape they would take. I lead and live a very drama-free, quiet, simple, and peaceful life now and would like it to remain that way. I will not go to your home, and I hesitate to ask you to bring Arnie to me, as I assume we have no desire to see each other. What options remain?

Arnie will always be my second favorite dog. My eyes are full of tears now as I type this. I do not know what to do. My only suggestion is do you have a friend willing to bring Arnie to me? Could you maybe meet me downtown somewhere and meet me again in two or three hours, after I've spent time with him? I am off work on Tuesday and Wednesdays currently. If you have any other suggestions, I would be open to them.

Sherrie: Jaz (my new puppy) has an hour obedience class at the pet store on Wednesdays from 2:00–3:00. I can bring Arnie there and leave him in the car while we are inside if you want to see him then. If not this Wednesday, it goes for another 4 weeks. Other than that, I don't know anyone who can bring Arnie downtown and then come and get him a few hours later.

Blake: Okay, I will let you know which Wednesday. Feels very sad. Like I have an hour to say goodbye. Guess I'll take it. Thanks.

Sherrie: Why goodbye? He's not on his last leg.

Blake: I understand. But, I see him now, then what? Am I missing something? There is no feasible way to do this on a regular basis, so it feels sort of . . . final. No?

Sherrie: I offered you the opportunity to see him. I have given you an alternative instead of coming to the house. If it's too painful for you to see him, then maybe you shouldn't see him. I don't know what else to say.

Blake: Aren't you just a wonderful person. So thoughtful as usual. Ya know what . . . thanks, but I think I will pass.

So, let's analyze this a bit. In the first long paragraph from Blake, I believe a normal response would be, "Great, what works for you?" Instead the passive-aggressive alcoholic/addict puts as much drama into his answers as Shakespeare. Also, Sherrie found it galling that he would ask her to seek out someone who would schlep Arnie downtown for a visit and then pick the dog up three hours later. Words are twisted and turned around as they don't coincide with what he wants, when he wants it. It really is a lose-lose situation. Almost no matter what Sherrie said or offered was good enough.

Ultimately, this dialogue went off course. What started as a simple conversation about a wonderful pet turned into a passive-aggressive conversation once the alcoholic/addict couldn't get his way. He turned the conversation back on Sherrie, though she was the one who offered a visit.

Typical passive-aggressive comments:

A passive-aggressive alcoholic/addict gets great pleasure in pointing out your faults and suggesting you can change and not be who you are. Here are some interesting exchanges and the comments made by someone with a passive-aggressive nature. There is a lack of compassion, and it comes on the heels not of anger, but as I said . . . this is a passive-aggressive exchange:

- You share your story of a difficult day at work or with another person. Their comment is, "You've had trouble before, so I'm not at all surprised."

- You share that something you did was good or appreciated. Their comment is, "You're always looking for a pat on the back or someone telling you how great you are."

- You share an opinion or thought on something. Their comment is, "You won't like that I disagree with you, so I'm not going to say anything."

- You share an idea that you are excited about or want to see through. Their comment is, "Why would anyone do that?" or "Who would ever think of doing that?"

- You share how you want to do something to improve

yourself or put yourself first for once. Their comment is, "You are one of the most self-centered people I know."

- You share that you are disappointed or angry at someone. Their comment is, "You're always resentful toward someone."

- You share a spur-of-the-moment exciting idea. Their comment is, "You never research or think things through."

- You share something that you decided to do your way. Their comment is, "You never listen to anyone."

Whether it's everyday communication, baiting and punishing, or dealing with a passive-aggressive nature, life with the alcoholic/addict can be challenging and quite exhausting. Not knowing where you stand or if your comments on anything will be disrespected, laughed at, or used to spark an avalanche of anger can and will keep anyone up at night.

After a while, even the most solid individual who habitually says, "I just let it roll of my back. It means nothing," will one day run out of this life with their hair on fire. In the worst case, they'll end up on one of those crime shows after killing the alcoholic/addict for not being able to tolerate one more furrowed eyebrow or verbal flogging.

Processing Questionnaire

- Is your dialogue with the alcoholic/addict going round and round and round?

- Are you finding that no matter what you say, you are always at fault?

- Does the alcoholic/addict take little or no responsibility for their actions?

- What are some phrases or words you can start to implement when the dialogue gets out of control or doesn't make sense anymore?

- What is your exit plan for when you are being baited and punished or just being used as a punching bag?

CHAPTER 9

ARE OTHERS JUDGMENTAL OF THE LOVED ONES OF ALCOHOLIC/ADDICTS?

As a columnist for the *Huffington Post* and *Psychology Today*, I am fortunate to be able to share some of my clients' issues with the public. I always keep my clients anonymous, but they have all said that if they can help others who may be experiencing something similar, then they are only too happy to see their stories posted.

At one of our sessions, my client Rita shared stories of her daughter's relapse. After the last relapse, she had made it clear to her daughter that she couldn't do anything more for her. Her daughter would be on her own and making all the decisions by herself if she relapsed again. Rita led me through not only the downfall but also some unsettling judgmental jabs from her family. After hearing the entire diatribe, I decided to post her story.

I received a number of thoughtful, caring comments and even more empathetic folks sent me emails sharing their own stories. I was grateful for the gentle guidance, suggestions, and encouragement. So many people opened their hearts and shared with me some obviously painful experiences. I shared these with Rita, and they made her feel validated about reinstating and reinforcing her boundaries.

So why am I writing about judgment? It seems that my blog hit some angry and old judgmental chords with Rita's family, and that is what I find interesting.

According to a number of dictionaries, a concise definition of "judgment" is *an authoritative opinion, a divine sentence or decision.* "Judgmental" is defined as *characteristics by a tendency to judge harshly. Denoting an attitude in which judgments about other people's conduct are made.* And so it was with some members of Rita's own family.

Rita's story

In an attempt to mend the frayed and brittle relationships between Rita and some family members, her brother-in-law (a crusader of trying to promote a happy, family atmosphere) decided to forward my blog. His intention was to try a different perspective regarding the journey Rita had taken with her daughter.

For years, her family members were privy to a stilted version regarding her involvement with the painful and dangerous situation of her daughter's substance abuse issues. Consequently, they formed their opinions and judgments with hearsay and didn't bother checking out all the facts.

Fast forward to a few weeks after her daughter's relapse, Rita's brother-in-law hoped the family might better understand the situation or her family might consider fresh information, which was different from what they had clung to for so many years. She had hopeful expectations of, "Wow, we didn't know that. Maybe we had judged her too harshly all those years." Instead this backfired with, "That's a bunch of crap. She has never been there for her child."

Rita felt sad that they still saw her back where she was over ten years ago. We spent quite a bit of time discussing the relationship a parent has with a child who is steeped in addiction and, therefore, engaging in self-destructive behavior. Most parents want to be there for their children. But what does that mean? I pondered what might be the answer to that question as a response to the recent barbs aimed at Rita's heart.

The interesting thing about this Q and A with family members is that when Rita posed these questions to them, they couldn't come up with an answer or solution. They kept saying that Rita was a lousy mother then and a lousy mother now.

Rita's daughter was active in her substance abuse and over twenty-one. So what was the answer? To have Rita's daughter move in with her so she could monitor her addiction, or lack thereof? To send her money every month on her promise that it was going to buy groceries or cat food and not drugs?

Could that be called responsible parenting? My definition of being there for one's alcoholic/addict child is encouraging your child to enter a sober living house or outpatient clinic and assuring your child that the finances could be worked out later. I would let my child know that I applauded any attempts made at living a clean and sober lifestyle. Ultimately, a good parent is one who encourages healthy decisions, not emotional ones.

Frankly, Rita didn't care anymore what those family members thought of her, but her brother-in-law was devastated. He is a nice man who saw an opportunity to bring a fragile, brittle family together. Too bad, he too was thrown under the bus.

Judgmental thinking

Judgmental thinking is the precursor to rescuing or enabling. The difference is that the rescuer or enabler is active in their participation. They want to physically change or get in there and take over that person's life because they don't approve of the path the alcoholic/addict or close family member is on.

In contrast, the person that stands in judgment of another can insulate themselves from physical involvement and only has to huff and puff from their soapbox about how wrong, uncaring, or selfish their prey is. Often they have no more facts about the situation than the man in the moon, but still they think they know best. If actions aren't taken to satisfy their interpretation, then under the bus they are thrown.

In addition, these judgments can last for years. No matter what the so-called culprit can do to rectify a situation, the die has been cast. Moving on or taking into consideration new disclosures are almost impossible for the one holding the judgment sword. It takes too much effort to be open to other possibilities. Since they have huffed and puffed about the shortcomings of this person for so long, their egos get in the way. Admitting that they were possibly wrong or now see a different angle is not in their wheelhouse of thinking.

Why are people so judgmental of others?

We all are judgmental in one way or another. I can find myself quietly judging why someone isn't more focused on achieving goals or doesn't watch what they eat. It's easy to cast dispersions, but maybe each of these individuals is doing the best they can to accomplish their goals, or maybe they just don't care. Frankly, what business is it of mine?

Making judgments about others can make someone feel superior. Usually, forming a one-sided opinion and lacking an empathetic heart is myopic thinking. We have heard the saying, "Before you criticize someone, you should walk a mile in their shoes." Very sophomoric for sure, but until one has stepped in another's shoes and seen their world through their eyes, they have no right to judge. It is mean and cruel and surely serves no purpose.

Processing Questionnaire

- Who is being judgmental of you?

- Why are they being judgmental?

- Have you approached this person and asked them why they are judging you and asked them to stop?

- If they feign ignorance about your request, what is your plan?

CHAPTER 10

How does one rebuild trust with the alcoholic/addict?

One of the most common discussions I have with my clients concerns when they can start trusting their loved one again. An enormous part of your loved one's recovery process and progress is built around them starting to pull themselves up by their own bootstraps. Making healthy decisions, weighing options, thinking through possibilities, and starting to rebuild their own life on life's terms all starts the repaving of the road of trust.

The more your loved one can come up with their own game plan, the more confidence will be built during their personal recovery as well as their addiction recovery. The alcoholic/addict needs to reconnect with themselves and start to trust their own core instincts for planning and developing a road map toward their goals. Even if you don't agree with the path they wish to take, or if ultimately it turns out to be the wrong path, let them be the lead Iditarod dog and be successful or not by their own doing.

CARD

Through the addiction process, an enormous amount of trust is broken. It follows that one of the first steps the recovering alcoholic/addict should commit to is starting to earn back the trust that was lost due to their addiction. We're talking not only about gaining your trust but also about the personal challenges in rebuilding their own trust of themselves.

I have created an acronym for what the family and friends of the alcoholic/addict should be witnessing as their recovery process strengthens. This acronym is "CARD."

C.A.R.D.

Credibility	= trustworthy
Accountability	= answerable for
Responsibility	= fulfilled obligation
Dependability	= reliable

These character traits are obviously interchangeable and joint. If the alcoholic/addict is living up to what these traits represent, then they are starting to become grounded and focused in recovery as well as life. These are actions of determination that are impossible to carry out on a regular or continued basis if they are in their addiction.

Through the addiction process, an enormous amount of trust is broken. The collective CARD acronym means "trust." When the credibility, accountability, responsibility, and dependability become everyday occurrences, then trust can start to be restored again.

In working with alcoholic/addicts, I've never encountered a client while in their addiction or in the first few months of recovery who has said yes when asked if they deserved to be trusted. They too realize that restoring trust takes time. If they are working on a solid, grounded recovery program, as well as enveloping life on life's terms, that trust will slowly but surely start to be restored among family members, friends, employers, and mates.

When in a sober state the alcoholic/addict can be reflective of what their irresponsible and out-of-control behavior was like and what they put others through because of their addiction. In an odd way they look forward to rebuilding that trust, for they want to prove to their loved ones as well as themselves that they are capable of being trusted once again. They genuinely want to be a good son, daughter, friend, or spouse to the ones they love. They desire to mend the past in which their family and friends were once so tormented by their addiction.

It's important for family and friends to give this process a substantial amount of time. At least six months of accountable, responsible behavior is needed, with no excuses for anything other than normal, minor infractions. In my practice I have often heard clients say that their son or daughter, husband or wife has been doing well, but this or that happened that wasn't their fault. They were unable to fulfill their promise or commitment because of someone else or due to circumstances out of their control.

If there is a legitimate issue where the bond of trust might be somewhat compromised, then fine. If not, then start your own clock of trust over again, and your loved one should do the same. There is nothing wrong with family or friends asking themselves periodically if their loved one is fulfilling the CARD program today.

In time your loved one will hopefully find their stride, reconnect with society, and prove to everyone around them, but most importantly to themselves, that they are restoring **c**redible, **a**ccountable, **r**esponsible, and **d**ependable behavior through their clean and sober lifestyle.

The recovering alcoholic/addict will revel in re-establishing that their word is now their bond. Like respect, trust is earned. And so far, they are on an accomplished path of recovery in more ways than one.

Processing Questionnaire

- How do you see your loved one rebuilding trust and responsibility?

- Are they really doing it on a consistent basis? Are you seeing circumstances the way you want to see them or how they really are?

- If your loved one has faltered with CARD, have you started the clock over?

- What does the new framework look like?

CHAPTER 11

WHAT IS IT LIKE TO DEAL WITH A LOVED ONE WHO IS AN ALCOHOLIC/ADDICT?

With permission from my clients, I have devoted a chapter to some of their stories and their trials and tribulations in loving the alcoholic/addicts in their lives. I sent out questions so they wouldn't stumble around looking for a place to start. Basically, I was looking for the following:

- What is the history of the person and the relationship?

- What was the disposition of this person before their struggle with addiction led to out-of-control behavior? (What traits did you fall in love with? What was your child like?)

- When did you first notice things were changing?

- How did you handle it? How did you approach the alcoholic/addict with what you saw?

- What was their response/action to your approach?

- What was the history of relapse/recovery if there was one?

- How successful was their recovery? Relapses?

- How was your relationship during this time period?

- Where are things today?

HUGH

My then wife and I adopted our beautiful baby daughter just minutes old. She had two adopted children from a first marriage who were living with us. Together we had already adopted another child five years earlier. We were thrilled about seeing our blended family grow, and we provided a comfortable, safe, and loving environment.

From an early age our second daughter, Tessa, was anxious, brooding, and not easy to please. We were aware of her history with an addicted birth mother, so we knew there might be some challenges as she grew up. We didn't care since we felt that by providing her with security and a respectful family life we could overcome anything.

As Tessa grew up and attended elementary school, it became clear that she was uncomfortable in her skin and that those around her were uncomfortable with her presence. Hence, this started the parade of therapists, counselors, tutors, and testing upon testing upon testing. Tessa wasn't stupid or slow, just lazy. If she didn't want to do something, she would ignite like a box of tinder.

Public school was no longer an option. She could not conform to any structure. She completed her junior high and high school education out of state at specialized schools that dealt with anger issues, cutting, eating disorders, and addiction. She had pieces of all this unhealthy pie.

Sadly, my relationship with her was strained since after several attempts at finding special schools, we found ourselves at odds with Tessa all the time. Our relationship was void of healthy conversations, and the blame game for her problems was always targeted for my heart. I remember one time visiting my daughter in a school in Texas only to spend literally five minutes in the counselor's office. When Tessa didn't like something I said, she got up and walked out, saying that I could leave and go home. I came and went in one day.

Many years later, nothing has changed much. We have had a few moments when the planets seem to align and we get along. But sadly, not for long. Like most alcoholic/addicts, if Tessa doesn't get what she wants from me when she wants it, she tells me what a horrible father I am. I am still the cause of her problems, and she asks why we adopted her and on and on.

JENNIFER

My daughter is the addict/alcoholic in my life. My father (her grand-father) and my brother were also alcoholics. My daughter has a mental health condition as well; she is bipolar with borderline personality disorder. With her family genetic history and her mental health issues, it was not too surprising she followed them in their addictions.

My daughter had depression at a very early age. I knew things weren't right, but she did well in school, was in sports, and was well liked. When she became a teenager, she changed. We thought this was just part of growing up and just what teenagers did at that point in their lives. We in no way condoned drinking or drugs, but you can't be with them all the time. We thought she would grow out of it. Later we found out her bipolar was adolescent onset. By the time she finished high school and went away to school, my husband had lost his job. This caused us to move to the house we had bought for our retirement and find a way to keep working for ten more years. We were in Arizona, and my daughter was in Pennsylvania. She got a job in a bar. Not long after that she was picked up for DUI leaving work. She had the option to spend time in jail or go to rehab on our dime. She chose rehab. She took it seriously and says it was one of the best things she has done. I believe she is off everything but marijuana. Not great, but that means her use is greatly scaled back, and it works for her anxiety.

Though she was off drugs and alcohol, all the problems that started her using were still there. We moved her to Arizona three times, but she missed her friends too much to stay. She was again picked up for DUI but under the influence of prescription drugs. She did not work for a couple of years. During this time I had tried to work with her to get her on disability. Finally, we advised her in December that we were no longer going to give her money if she would not go to work or follow up on disability. She did get a job and has been working since January. Her life is the most normal I have seen since she lived at home. Aging/maturing seems to be helping her. Her favorite show is Dr. Phil, which is funny since he works with people like her all the time. He tells it like it is, which she likes.

She wants to live in Arizona again. We are moving toward that, but she will not be living with us. We know living with us does not work. We'll see how it works out.

EDWARD

I met my wife at a birthday party. She was vibrant and full of life with striking blue eyes and an engaging smile. Needless to say I was attracted from the get go. After a few dates, I found her to be pretty hot headed and sometimes a bit irrational, but the strong passionate side kept winning me over.

In looking back over those early years, I can recall some very chaotic and confusing moments when her behavior could turn into physical violence toward me. I didn't notice (or maybe I didn't want to notice) that many of these outbursts were ignited by too much alcohol.

I don't know exactly when I entertained the thought that my now wife might be an alcoholic. We both enjoyed going out with friends, and drinking was a part of our lives then and for the next twenty years.

For the most part, beer was a constant for both of us. We either went out or hung out at the house and enjoyed drinking with friends or just by ourselves on a regular basis. I never thought either of us had a problem with drinking, certainly not to the point of dependency. However, many people would say we drank way too much and would go further, and had anyone made a prediction about one of us becoming an active alcoholic even I would have assumed it would have been me.

My wife became pregnant and we welcomed twin sons into our life. She suffered from postpartum depression, and it seemed like her drinking did increase. The addition of children in our lives, while the most amazing thing imaginable, brought much pressure and stress for us both and perhaps served as the catalyst for our first venture to couples therapy. Neither of us got much out of it, but she had basically told me she wanted a divorce. Even though I don't think we achieved much, we did retire to our separate corners to sulk, but did not divorce. Damage was definitely done. We were not openly hostile with one another, but we were not carefree with each other either. A year or so passed, and I think for the most part we got along okay and carried on. The big change came when she started suggesting we have another child. We ended up back in therapy. All the old stuff came back up, and I expressed my fears openly that I was genuinely scared our own relationship was just beginning to recover. I did not want to risk us adding a third child in our lives. It was four years and month after the twins were born that our third child came into this world.

During the second pregnancy my wife had taken to allowing herself a glass of red wine every once in a while. That was thirteen years ago. I do know that her taste for wine became stronger than the taste for beer. It got her drunk more quickly, and there did seem to be more nights when she was stumbling more often, but it was gradual and nothing too dramatically different. Then there nights when we would come home from being out and instead of coming to bed she would go out on the deck and drink on her own. I know at first I would get angry (not outwardly but inwardly) that she was staying out on the porch drinking because the window of opportunity for intimacy was getting shorter and shorter. Sometimes she would come on to bed and all was well, but then other times she would pass out in the living room.

So the way I started to realize my wife had a drinking problem was because my desire to be with her was being met less and less. Still I would not have said she was an alcoholic. My irritability with the dissatisfaction in our personal lives was definitely now getting in the way of our relationship in the (many) non-drinking hours. I was cold and hostile on the morning after. Never once did I say why or openly tell her I missed being able to be with her. Other relationships were suffering too.

At this point in our relationship we barely touched anymore, and I know I was extremely frustrated at her for being "shut out." I definitely had a part in the lack of intimacy. I was unable to speak to her about it, and instead felt resentment toward her for not being available to me anymore. I honestly don't know if I still loved her when this was happening. One moment she is telling me she wants a divorce and she is telling me I am always calling her a horrible person. Honestly even though I could spin it that this was the moment I knew my wife was an alcoholic, I still was not convinced of it.

One day after what seemed unusually heavy drinking for her (when there was some peace between us), I quietly said I was worried that she seemed to be drinking a lot more. This was received in the manner I gave it. She was not angry. She was appreciative and glad of my concern and echoed that she had recently realized that ever since she switched from mostly beer to mostly wine she drank more than she wanted and got drunk more often and passed out more often. So openly this was the first time I really registered there was a problem and shared it with her appropriately.

A period of attempting to slow down or maybe stop began. She would say she would drink only on the weekends or maybe just one glass of wine per night. For the most part I had no hand in this. She would say what she was going to do, then would either follow through or not depending on how she was doing. Once again she tried to ease up on her drinking. My wife seemed more anxious all the time. She would do okay for a few days, or that was what it looked like to me. Even though it looked like she maybe was drinking less, her behavior was more and more erratic.

I call this my dark period because I started to think in some codependent way to feel I was trapped, and my life was basically a huge mess, and it was all because of her, and I was completely helpless. I started to look for an exit strategy. So I started to think maybe if she would bottom out and have to go into rehab, then I could leave her and no one could blame me. She did end up in rehab, but it took several more months.

Round one of rehab started with me feeling I had finally scored a point for sobriety in our home. I was advised early on regarding my wife's treatment, "You know this is just the beginning. Even if she comes home sober, there is lots of work to do." It did burst my bubble a bit, but in hindsight I say thank God. I would have gone to pick my wife up on the day of release with this great expectation that I would be picking up a completely different person than the one I had dropped off. While she looked so much better, her face was much less swollen, and she seemed to be so much happier, things were extremely strained between us.

Lots of family and friends were saying she really should stay a lot longer, saying you know the longer they are in the better the chance of them staying sober longer becomes. I have no point of reference to refute or prove that statement. Anyway, home she came. It got ugly again quickly. She came home a seriously dry drunk, hateful of me and maybe herself, but a whole lot of anger toward me. My wife would enter rehab three more times from this day.

Going on forty days sober since her last visit to rehab, it is hard for me to trust our relationship. For that reason, it has gone backwards. I can look at my part and say I have definitely begun to put up walls,

I am tired and lonely and want her back in my life, but I'm scared to reach out as I feel I may be attaching myself to a sinking ship. All the while knowing that even though she should be able to ride this out, we both create a wake. If I am not careful I can inadvertently create enough wake to sink her ship, and she can do likewise.

The trick is for me to learn how to stop circling her and to reengage with her. Right now I am finding that very hard. Why do I hang in here and keep trying? I feel like if I can stop myself being cautious and overly self protective, learn to take care of myself and yet not be a disruption to those most important in my life, then I can gain a life back that I am truly connected to. Right now I am just not connected to it because I am so afraid of getting hurt again.

I do know I am in a process of change, and it is really hard for me to effect change on myself. I am just not the best person to stop and ask myself what is it I really want or need. I find it hard to be honest with myself because I often literally don't even know what it is that motivates me or keeps me going. I do know I have tried extremely hard to be as absolutely honest with myself in what I have written here. Understanding where I did well and where I failed myself and my wife are an integral part of the process.

Just before Thanksgiving of this year, my wife had a slip; she came to me full of guilt and told me she had been drinking again. I was able to direct her back to her sponsor in A.A. and not engage myself in trying to resolve the conflict she was having. At the same time I was also better able to say to myself should she not be able to self-correct, I was not about to go down the old road of relapse and detox again. One slip turned into a couple of weeks, and the roller coaster of anger and resentment toward herself and me started all over again. She has attempted yet again another rehab, but it has forced me to redirect my thoughts once again to, "Why am I here, and where would I like to be?" I know I still love her, but I also know I do like myself enough to not put myself back in the mess again.

It's kind of scary, but I have had a few of those moments again over the last couple of days where I have found extreme peace despite the chaos. There have been moments when the anxiety is running rampant, but nothing like it did three or four years ago. The truth is I do love my wife (not the behavior she exhibits when active or in denial), and over the last five years there have been moments when the person I fell in love with is apparent. When in sobriety, she can be extremely aggressive still and irrational, but I am so much better equipped to handle that now than I used to. When active, there is not much room for a relationship. I start to withdraw under the barrage of open hostility. What I am beginning to see is that I don't always have to withdraw and I don't always have to fight.

Who knows what tomorrow will bring. I will turn my will and care over to my Higher Power and pray for my family for peace, love, and respect, starting with giving myself permission to respect myself more and more. The more I do that the better I become at being able to navigate my way through the challenges that come my way. I can't say with 100 percent assurance that we will work things out; however, it does seem the clearer I become about what it is I want our relationship to look like and can actually express that openly and honestly, the more it does seem to be a possibility (at least to me).

It seems to be about my ability to stand up for myself, to not accept (or rather not take on board) the irrational behavior. There is more clarity for me now more than ever that with or without drinking our relationship is a challenge, but that for it to be viable it is critical for the drinking to come to an end. The most peaceful and respectful moments of the years since the time I first acknowledged my wife as an alcoholic have definitely been when she has been actively engaged in recovery and is not actively drinking.

Today she is active (heavily active), and things are rough. Should she elect to get back engaged in recovery, I think we have a great shot at staying married. Should she elect not to reengage in recovery, I would say the chances are slim. Perhaps I have no say in this ultimately, but I do know that should she not be able to reengage in recovery, I don't have to stay if I don't want to.

ALISE

I fell in love with my husband very quickly. He was different from the other men I was accustomed to. That was just it: He was a man, not some guy playing at being a man. He took his work seriously. He pursued me with such passion and fervor. He swept me off my feet.

I was a bit of a party girl when we got together. I enjoyed going out, drinking, dancing, and having a blast. I was in full party-mode when I met my husband. For the first few months, we enjoyed "party-mode" together. This became less amazing the deeper in love we became, so we ended up partying at home, where other people couldn't interfere with our bubble. What would have been drinks out before dinner turned into a drink on the sofa before dinner. Then, we were just drinking at home.

I gained an enormous amount of weight from drinking until heavily intoxicated before eating a family dinner. Instead of dancing after drinking like a party girl, I would sit and watch *The Crocodile Hunter* with my fiancé, the dinner weighing me down, followed by a few more cocktails.

I didn't mind the weight gain like I would now. I had blinders on to how my physique was deteriorating in addition to how unhealthy our routines were. We continued this course of bringing a single, party-style drinking into a committed relationship lifestyle. Although we were fairly active, most of our activities included drinking.

One of our favorite activities was camping. We have an enchanted camping spot that we tried to get to every chance we had. As soon as we arrived, the drinks were poured. At first, this was just a fun way to unwind. After we were married, camping became less of a fun time and more of a trip into my husband's own personal alcoholic stage production.

On the way to the campground, he would insist that I make him an excessively large (42-ounce) vodka soda right away. He packed the car so that the cocktail makings were at the top, readily accessible. I hated his drink cup. It was bright orange with cheerful beach scenes on it, a plastic lid that secured tightly, and a straw. It could hold half a bottle of vodka. It symbolized the start of him instigating drunken interactions with other campers who were unfortunate enough to make eye contact or say a friendly word as they happened by. At this campground, campers did drink, and heavily, but most of the heavy drinkers were college kids. As evening wore on, the orange cup would have a refill and the interactions with other campers would become more caustic. It became humiliating for me. Sometimes I wished the ground would swallow me up. I would watch his disconjugate gaze swim with malice in the campfire toward the next set of approaching voices, try to engage his attention elsewhere, then just watch his next encounter of harsh, discombobulated lashing out fall upon the unsuspecting folk trying to enjoy their evenings.

I felt small, unimportant, ashamed, degraded, alone, afraid, and brokenhearted. Mostly, I felt helpless. I wanted to help my husband more than anything else in the world—including winning the lottery. I wanted to get back to that place of blissful love that we had at the beginning, before the vortex of booze swallowed him whole. There were times at night when he would be drunk, unreachable, and so far away from me even though he was sitting right next to me, that I thought I would never get him back. Sometimes, I felt lost in the despair.

My husband was not willing to make changes with his drinking, so I persevered with changes in my own life. I decided to carry on with my education and pursued my teaching credential and masters degree. I consulted a doctor about my weight. This doctor prescribed some medication to help with the weight loss, along with my walking and yoga. The only caveat was that alcohol could not be consumed with the medication. This was fine with me. When I quit drinking, I really realized how much my husband was drinking. When my weight-loss doctor asked how it was going, I was very up-front with her. She referred me to a counselor who helps with the families of addicts.

My counselor saved my relationship with my husband. I didn't know what I was doing or how to help myself, much less my husband. After working with her for a while, I developed coping skills and language that empowered me to reclaim my life. We came up with a plan to get my husband to work with her as well. It was a long process that took dedication and a few different "plans" for my husband to cut back.

One plan had him not drinking on the weekends. That worked for two months. Another plan switched him off vodka to wine. That lasted a little longer. He went back to vodka eventually. His drinking increased to the point that his liver functions were concerning to his doctor. Nothing seemed to get his attention enough to quit.

Then Michael Jackson died. It isn't that the King of Pop gave up the ghost; I just remember that it happened the same day my husband was arrested for driving under the influence. He hadn't been drinking that day, just speeding. There was so much booze in his system that his over-taxed liver couldn't process it out. A deal-breaker that I have and have stuck to vehemently is that I won't be with a person who drinks and drives. Although I take my marriage vows seriously, my husband understood that he was narrowly escaping a heartbreaking divorce by not having had a drink that day. It was a wake-up call for him. We made very big changes.

The first thing we did was leave our toxic lifestyle. We sold our home, packed our car, including the cat, and took off across the country. We found a rehab in Little Rock where my husband found humility, sobriety, and brotherhood. The A.A. meetings across the country were a welcoming thread of humanity. He didn't have any relapses. Once he was done, it has never been an option to go back.

The economy collapsed at the same time that this major shift in our lifestyle occurred, but we don't have children or major responsibilities. We were able to truly start over. Moving from South Carolina to Chicago was a massive change that provided stability for a newly sober spouse. It was away from all of the previous triggers and enablers.

We decided to move back to South Carolina after suffering through two-and-a-half years of Chicago weather and Midwestern terseness. My husband's eleven-hour working days were done. After nine months being back, my husband found a job working at home.

This is where things get strange. I have always had the burdens of making the difficult choices in our relationship. In fact, I am used to being "the decider" for everything. Having a loving, supportive, wonderful husband at home to help with things takes getting used to. I am not a team player. It isn't that I don't want to be. I have longed for it with every fiber of my being. Passing on things that I had to keep an incredibly tight rein on is difficult!

Living together like normal people is amazing, but it is taking some getting used to.

SUSAN

At one point or another in the world of alcoholism, you realize you are living the lie that envelops it all, not recognizing the subtle beginning of the problems to come.

Everything appeared under control, and for many years it was, being a very much in-control social drinker, I never had any issues with alcohol. About ten years ago that's when a few things changed, and unbeknownst to me, would begin to change our world. Out of nowhere, I had a spouse beginning to use alcohol out of control before my very eyes, medicating himself from the frustration of a part of our life not in the plan, everything spiraled out of control, affecting every single one of us watching it happen. It became the fear of what would happen next and when. We tried talking as a family only to have episode after episode shocking us all each time with heartbreak.

For twenty-five years we had the marriage others would say was pretty close to perfect. We truly loved each other and had our fairy-tale life planned out years in advance as to how things were to go, or so we thought. We planned when we would get married, when we would start a family, where we would live, and in what school district we would be in by that time for our kids to start Kindergarten.

My husband was in complete control of everything, always and for everyone it seemed at times. I was blissfully content being a homemaker and a mother. We walked through life with all our plans just falling into place with my husband surprising me with wonderful things at every bend in the road. When we needed a place to take our kids in the winter, he bought us a home on the ocean in Florida, when the kitchen got too small where we spent our summers at the lake with his family, he bought me a beautiful home of my own down the street. Nothing ever seemed to go wrong with him in charge. We appeared to have it all, and in many ways we did. Together, the only plan was to build our lives together, build our family, and continue life in this wonderful way we had created. I scratched my head at people who had marriages that didn't make it. For years I wondered how couples could get so out of sync. I had a trust in him that would scare me at my young age. How could I ever live without him, I often shuddered. We had so much in common, it worked, and we had enough differences that complimented it all.

This instability that came into our lives took me years to believe was happening and even more years to understand—unfortunately, even longer to admit to myself. I hated when our then-grown kids would use the words "drunk" or "alcoholic." I just didn't want to hear them; that was never the man I knew. I tried everything to make it all go away: going to doctors, acupuncturists, therapists; clearing the house of alcohol, monitoring where he went, following him around, chasing him down, plotting and planning—to never win the battle of it all around me. I tried the old "if you can't beat 'em join 'em" by having a drink with him and controlling where he went and how much he had that way, or so I thought. Getting rid of his bad-influence friends that had the same habits. I can't think of anything I didn't try on a daily or weekly basis to make this nightmare go away. Never understanding the entire time it wasn't my problem to fix. I was certainly the fixer. I could fix everything. Why couldn't I fix this? We found big bottles, little bottles, everywhere; there was no place he didn't try to hide it. It took me some time in the race of covering, hiding, and lying to myself before I had to admit this was actually happening, and then, even with that, it still wasn't the end.

Denial is huge in this world, and it starts with oneself. I didn't want to admit we had a problem in our healthy appearing four walls. There was nothing we couldn't solve. How could we have any problems now? And this would surely go away today. Today would be better. He would snap out of it all. I began to sit at the window at five p.m. and wait to see how the car would drive in after work, straight down the drive or over the curb. Day after day, I would worry of what was going to be coming home at five o'clock, to the point I started to get my own anxiety issues in it all. Family gathering after family gathering, holiday season after holiday season, these were huge stressful times, for what was to happen then, and how were we going to deal with this person who won't admit for one minute to having a problem. I was watching a loved one become so sick and not being able to do a thing about it. Alcohol had a hold we couldn't seem to break free from.

Finally, an OWI (Operating While Intoxicated). Thank goodness, that would teach him for sure, and it did for a while, But not so fast, not even that was enough. For we were used to buying our way out, getting our way around, and beating the system for so long, we soon figured out how to do that here as well. Our way of dealing with stress had a hold. This would sit on his shoulder telling him on a daily basis that a drink would help make things better, that they were all wrong and just one drink would be okay. And off to the races we would go again and again. I often wondered how could someone so incredibly smart be so stupid here.

I prayed for change, cried to whomever would listen and could help us as we continued to fall through the cracks of the control it had on our family. Years passed and I grew madder and began to even get cold and hateful to what he was doing to the family we had made. After years of battling someone else's problem, I enjoyed the days when he would be at work, then at five o'clock it would be over and reality would smack me in the face yet again. How bad would it be? Would he be intoxicated driving in? Or would he try to sneak once he got here? I never knew what to expect. The only thing I could count on was being disappointed.

After losing my mother to cancer and my father to grief, the sadness helped me become strong and realize my life was more important than putting up with all this. I would scream at the top of my lungs in the bathtub. How could I be losing the three most important people in my life in twenty-four months? I cried the last year of my mother's life; unbeknownst to me, instead of having happy times she heard me so beside myself and depressed. Moving along not giving his problem as much thought, I worked through loss more important to my heart in losing my mother and the strength I needed to walk through that. I began to become stronger. In it all, I set dates as to when I was done dealing with someone else's problem.

By that time, and finally by my birthday when I turned fifty-five, I was done. I had had several friends who were miserable and divorcing in their sixties. I thought, I am not waiting that long. If this is what I have to deal with, then so be it, I will deal with it now. I began to make a plan; I looked at small, quaint houses I could live in unafraid, where my kids and grandchildren could enjoy our new life. I made a plan for myself and my future, thinking that if I had a plan, then I wouldn't be so devastated by any surprise. I had already thought things out just in case. When times would get bad, I would think of my plan, lay in bed with my eyes closed, and dream of how it would be, as if I were walking through a dream. With all that, I knew I would be okay. We struggled through the times with our kids, being done with all this every time dad would put them through so much stress and worry, teaching them with each time how to get a thicker skin toward alcoholism. Perhaps easier for them I thought, or I hoped, for they're building their lives with someone else. Mine was to have been mapped out. Now what was there left for me? Time after time, we would reason, fight, and cry about what had to be to go on together.

For the first time ever, he did something completely unlike him: he left to stay in a hotel with the excuse of needing time to think, hopeful for the possibility on our end it could be a light at the end of the tunnel we had prayed for. Disappointingly, this happened three times in five months, disappearing and not letting anyone know where he was. His biggest enabler and the most in denial was his mother. Eventually calling after days, each time wanting to come back home, sick from lack of care for himself and any constraints of his alcohol intake. He would come back to where I could hide things enough that he would be forced into detox, and then would be sick and up all night with apologies of his unacceptable behavior upon his arrival, knowing down deep this was killing him, wanting it to stop, and beginning the road of getting away from it again.

The last time I went through this, I knew it was getting closer to the end for me; I started making a plan in my mind of what my life would be away from all this stress. I planned what my house would look like, and I put it on my computer as my background. I planned what would I do and how would I live. I knew I would be okay, feeling like I would just pour my heart into my family, cooking for them, and watching my grandchildren, and that would give me comfort and direction. He began to try to start fights with me to leave to go to our lake home alone, only to get a multitude of calls wondering why I wasn't in the car heading up behind him. That happened twice. The second time I finally told the kids I couldn't protect them any longer from their father and what he may do. I told them that if they chose to go to the lake, they know what they may have, and if they didn't want to be around that, then they shouldn't go, because I am not going. It started an incredible uproar and a tremendous amount of phone calls from him over and over telling me all about the family time happening that I was missing out on, and how dare I not be there for it all. I heard all about their plans, how much fun they were having, and what they were doing next—all untrue, for on the other side, the kids were texting me telling me they weren't talking to him. He sat in the same chair on the porch all weekend, with them just walking past him.

Lies are the norm. I know that now, and a drinker has many lies to tell, to the point the truth is fleeting—running so fast you can barely ever find it. As I stayed at home enjoying the peace and quiet of not having the stress around me that summer weekend, I decorated our balcony in our home for me to sit out there and relax and leave my stress behind. Every level of our home was torn up for renovating. I never could decide whether this added to my stress or gave me a way to keep my mind off of it, so a peaceful place was hard to find. I spent Friday night and Saturday thinking about my life and how I wanted to live it. Being away from the problem made me finally realize I didn't want to be around it, for this distance was calming and educational as well. The person I loved my whole life with my whole heart was teaching me how to fall out of love with him. I had cried all my tears, so while searching the Internet for design ideas, I would also search for a little more self-help for myself and my family.

All of a sudden out of nowhere was a book that in all my searching I had never seen before. I felt as though my mother in heaven had helped me find it. I read through the pages and came upon a number to call for more counseling help, not understanding what that meant. Spending the rest of my weekend alone in the peace and quiet, I relaxed in deep thought. On Sunday morning while having coffee in bed, the phone rang with an apology of not getting back to me the day before. I was shocked that at the other end of the phone was the author herself. Carole Bennett was calling me? That was the counselor? We chatted for a few minutes and set up a time to talk further, I began to learn to do just as the title of the book says to do: reclaim your life. I began to reclaim mine. I thought if I could have figured out the magic way after all this time I would have, so I had to trust someone smarter than I was in this entire situation, so I did everything she told me to do. Calling with any snags, I set forth a plan, not knowing what the end would look like but knowing enough that now there would be change. I halted my other counselor and only listened to Carole. I walked through the guided steps of my life towards hope for a better future for me with a plan for everything that could happen.

One day when talking to Carole about the "what to do ifs," she asked me, "Didn't you tell me you had a bag packed in your car?"

I said, well, yes.

And Carole said, "Well, take the damn thing out of your car because you're not going to do a thing!"

She calmed me down by saying, "That's okay. You don't have to. You can live just like you are."

But it rustled my feathers enough for me to make a move. It was the right amount and the right time for tough love that I needed to hear. I began to pack and plan. I had no clue for how long and to where I would be going, but unpredictable is what I needed to be. I had to set a different path for me and shake up anything for a slight hope of change, but for certain change for myself. I told the kids what I was doing, gave them my emergency only phone number, and as instructed, I wrote a note to leave behind for my husband. I went to a friend's place, where I hid my car, to gather my thoughts and make plans to leave the state where he couldn't find me.

After a few days of rest, I got in my car and drove to New Mexico to spend time with my sister. As I turned on to the entrance to the interstate heading west, my mind was racing trying to figure out what this at-home mom was doing. On the easy listening station, I had been listening to a gospel song with the right words I needed to hear played, all about doing the right thing by yourself, and the right time to do it and that God is helping you the whole way. Over and over I sang the repetitive words through my tears as I drove with my dog right beside me; with my buddy I would never be alone. I had to go to see what we would have in the dust that settled, if anything. Nine days followed with no communication, and after that time was reentry. I talked to Carole as I drove toward town with a "Dear God, what do I do next?"

Reentry, what was that going to look like? I definitely had woken someone up, and he did see a new strength in me that he believed would carry me through what I had to do. And for the first time, he had to turn around and decide if he wanted to lose all of us to this way of life. Six long years we went through this, and I stuck to my guns from my birthday being the day I would not go past, to move on with time running out. I had laid down a new understanding for my life and what I was willing to live around.

Initially after I got home, he was sick for days detoxing. I said that I would help one last time, but this would be the last time I ever helped with this part; and I barely did—even videotaping him to later view how sick he really gets, for he must forget. That has been several months now, and stumble, yes he has. For the first time, stubborn as he can be, he is seeing that to keep his family he has to reclaim his own life and become the healthy person he was for so many years before. It's not always easy, as all who have battled demons in our lives know. Everyone has them on some level, and I have worked on mine all my life, for self-help has always interested me. Everyone goes on that journey differently in their life and decides when change is right. It was right for me.

I thank God for a good ending to this story. It is still a work in progress, but it is now work being done in the right direction instead of the wrong. The plan is to continue on our path to finding our lives again, my security in it all is trust, learning to trust again, but more importantly, to trust in myself knowing I am strong, knowing that someone else isn't going to determine my happiness, and a substance isn't going to control my destiny.

Many hugs to all the women going through this; I know the shoulder you need. Stand tall and stay strong for yourself. Reach out and find that someone you need to say the right thing to at the right time that wakes you to make a change. Change is good. Change is healthy, and change is up to you, that I know now. Forever grateful.

I am deeply grateful to these clients for sharing their very personal stories with you, the reader. It took not only an enormous amount of time but also great soul searching and digging up of some very painful experiences. It is a huge sisterhood and brotherhood out there, and I'm hopeful that you can relate to a portion, if not all, of these stories.

Processing Questionnaire

- Did any of these stories ring true for you?

- If so, what could you most relate to?

- Are you ready to try journaling your personal story for your own self?

CHAPTER 12

Is it possible to move on toward a healthier tomorrow?

There are many things that inhibit us from moving on. Usually our inhibitions are fear-based since the unknown can be terrifying. Sadly, we would rather stay and be comfortable with the devil we know than take the chance of making a change. Sometimes that change can happen overnight and not of our doing; other times tons of thought goes into weighing the pros and cons of what we are contemplating. Being honest with ourselves is the first step. Often I will tell my clients that it's okay to live with the alcoholic/addict as long as they don't pretend to live in a dream world or hope magically that something might change. Sometimes things or situations do demand change, but usually life goes on day by day as it has for years.

However, there is a point when someone finally looks in the mirror and realizes they can't take the situation anymore. They realize that if they don't do something to change their life, then they truly will become a shell of themselves, and that's really no way to live. Fear has a very, very strong grip on us. Sometimes we are glued to more unhealthy reasons to stay in an abusive or unfulfilling relationship than reasons to move on. If we tell ourselves that making the change can't make life any worse than it already is, then maybe that will spur us on to take the plunge and trust the outcome. After all, one can always go back to their personal dungeon, but I am almost 100 percent certain that that won't happen.

Personal passion

So what are some of the ways that we can personally move on to grasp a healthier tomorrow? In going through some of my personal journeys, especially the beginning of the unraveling of my marriage to the alcoholic, I realized that it was the beginning of planting the tiny seeds for a healthier tomorrow.

Years ago I was interested in writing a book about the pain and suffering the family of the alcoholic/addict goes through and endures on an almost daily basis. It doesn't matter who is suffering—spouse, child, parent, or sibling—frustration, anger, and confusion all run rampant. I decided to write a book about the roller coaster life I was experiencing with my husband, who clearly had a drinking problem. Whether it was going to get published or not, it was my first foray into gaining my own dignity and respect back. When he discovered what I was doing, he constantly questioned my motives for writing the book and often made comments like, "What do you know about addiction?"; "Maybe you should just make this a pamphlet"; and "Nobody's going to read anything like this."

He tried constantly to clip my wings of confidence, but with every snip his comments did just the opposite and moved me further ahead. Each day that I wrote my book I was becoming empowered by my newfound passion. I knew that for my passion to see this book through I had to have a plan, an outline for my thoughts, and an end goal. I persevered over years and earned a degree in Clinical Psychology, working in the world of addiction and recovery. I starting to outline what I wanted to say. Years later, *Reclaim Your Life: You and the Alcoholic/Addict* was born. I'm pleased that this tiny seed of a thought turned into a full-blown passion that has helped folks all over the world understand their loved one's addiction issues and their own part in the alcoholic/addict's life.

Finding a personal passion is one of the key concepts for healthy growth and development. Passions are a very personal journey. If you pick the right one (and even if you don't, try, try again), you can revel in the private experience you are sharing with the most important person in the world, yourself.

Goals and deadlines can be important if that helps keep you on track, but putting too much pressure on yourself to rebuild the best

Mustang around or write the next great American novel may deflect you from the purpose of self-fulfillment. Find your personal passion, regardless of the outcome, even if there is nothing tangible to show at the end of the day. Stirring up the intellect by taking some interesting classes on world history or whatever your area of interest can be construed as a bona fide passion. Thinking about your passion and planning on how you see it develop is an excellent start. When I decided to write my book there were more nights than not that I would sit and stare at the computer screen. "Jump right in. Come on, the water's great" kept playing over and over in my head. Ego can be a great foe that whispers in your ear, "You can't do this. Who do you think you are?" It became a job in and of itself to shut that negative yapping off.

It's a challenge to push ourselves in another direction. We have to take away our thinking that has been on the same wavelength for many years. "I have no time; I don't know what I'm doin'" can be a constant mantra. But as the percolation for the desire to write a book turned into a full rolling boil, I committed to sitting down and transcribing every note I had taken, every memory I had stored, and all the sessions in which my clients shared the private hell they were going through.

From scores of journals and miles of taped sessions with clients, my book was finally on its way. My passion turned into a desperate desire to be of service to others experiencing the same hell I once had. To this day, the small seed of passion was watered, cultivated, and given plenty of sun and air to grow strong . . . and grow tall and strong it did.

Taking your daily inventory

Let's now look at how we can move toward a healthier tomorrow and build a life that is self-containing. One way that I have found helpful is in taking a daily inventory, or as I like to do, check in with myself. Many of my clients do nothing but talk about the alcoholic/addict in their life. Their world is centered on the alcoholic/addict and their behavior toward themselves and others. How they cope or deal with their situation becomes such a primary focus for them that often they lose their own commitment to the task at hand.

So what do I mean about checking in with yourself? Twice a day, I ask myself, "What's wrong, what's right, or good or bad, or

150   CAROLE BENNETT, M.A.

unsettling or uncomfortable?" I find that when I can be specific about what's bothering me and say it out loud on a walk with my dogs, I can process it with more clarity and focus. I can also ascertain if it's really worth much thought or if it is something pretty minor just bothering me at the moment.

Here's how my script reads:

Me: "What's wrong?"

My answer: "I'm not happy/worried/concerned about . . ."

Becky — My friend Becky didn't call me back in a timely fashion.

Larger monthly expenses — I'm anxious about finances this month as I had car and household repairs that were very expensive.

Bridge partner — I have no bridge partner for the week.

Communication with the alcoholic — I'm distressed that I thought I was making progress communicating with the alcoholic in my life only to find out that he's really the same dysfunctional person as always. Nothing's changed.

What's important about processing what I'm not happy about is the next question I ask:

Me: "Can I do something to change my attitude?"

My answer: "I can think more positively and upbeat . . ."

Becky — Let it go and maybe she will call, text, or communicate with a good reason as to why she has not gotten back to me. Also, I want to make myself aware that these are my expectations and time frame, so it's not fair to impart them on another. In all honesty, how important is it?

Larger monthly expenses — Well, life is life. Unfortunately, they have piled up on top of one another all at one time, but stuff just needs fixing.

Bridge partner — I'll make some calls or plan for something else that day. Work on my new book, volunteer at the zoo, etc. . . .

Communication with the alcoholic — Unfortunately, nothing new there. All I can do is be patient and maybe something will transpire. Just keep praying for their well-being; that's all I can do.

Back to my script:

Me: "What's right?"

My answer: "I'm happy and grateful that none of my friends or family are ill (nor am I, for that matter). I received a nice order for my catering company. I live in paradise. I surround myself with wonderful animals."

I don't need to dissect the good like the bad. I just need to bring it to my attention.

Nightly recap

At the end of the day, I go through a recap to see if the bit of annoying negativity has changed at all. Oftentimes it has, or I have a different outlook on it. Maybe I don't care when my friend calls me back, or maybe I can make plans to go sailing on the day I was going to play bridge, so I'm excited for the new adventure.

Most things that I check in with myself about are not enormous, life-altering decisions; though I have found this exercise works just as well. If I can't seem to scrape the gum off my shoe regarding a situation that is really bothering me, or if I can't seem to shake it or find an answer for it, I turn my thoughts over to what I call "A Memo From God."

I appreciate that I have a co-pilot (God or whomever you are comfortable believing in) helping me with my issues. The key for me is to turn the wheel over to my Higher Power, totally and unencumbered, and then step back and let the chips fall where they may.

Memo from God

Here is a "memo" that circulated through my practice years ago, and I still find it very helpful and, of course, timeless.

To: YOU
Date: TODAY
From: GOD
Subject: YOU
Reference: LIFE

This is God. Today I will be handling all of your problems for you. I do NOT need your help. So, have a nice day. I love you.

PS: And remember, if life happens to deliver a situation to you that you cannot handle, do NOT attempt to resolve it yourself! Kindly put it in the SFGTD (something for God to do) box. I will get to it in MY TIME. All situations will be resolved, but in MY TIME, not yours. Once the matter is placed into the box, do not hold onto it by worrying about it. Instead, focus on all the wonderful things that are present in your life now.

Should you decide to send this to a friend, thank you. You may have touched their life in ways you will never know!

Now, you have a nice day.

God

God has seen you struggling.

God says it's over.

Touching base with ourselves is significant in keeping our resentments down to a low roar. As I said, when we can talk to ourselves on a walk, in the shower, or wherever we're comfortable, then our thinking and worrying doesn't have time to build up, fester, and become larger than life.

One last thought: Be kind to yourself when you are running through the ups and downs of the moment. This is not about woulda, shoulda, coulda, or Monday morning quarterbacking. It's just a simple and honest check-in to see how the day is starting out and how it ended.

Many of my clients as well as myself are older and have wonderful life experiences that have been safely tucked away in our memories. We no longer worry about getting our first job, starting a family, changing careers, or making decisions that we might have considered in our twenties, thirties, and forties. We are getting older and loving it because there are a lot of benefits that can come with our wrinkles, which are like rings on a tree.

No one looks forward to getting older, but if we are lucky, it will happen. It's certainly better than the alternative. I have often been asked if I could be twenty or thirty again, would I? Like most folks, I would probably say yes only if I could take the knowledge I have accumulated over all these years back with me.

I had a big birthday this past January, and I celebrated with some gal pals over a lavish dinner. I stated "no gag gifts please" as I didn't want boxes of Depends, hemorrhoid cream, laxatives . . . well, you get the picture. One of the highlights of the evening was going around the table and all taking part in reminiscing about our lives, what we have learned, what we would change, and where we see our futures.

My children are grown and live about an hour away. They have their busy lives, as do I. I am single but live with my two Golden Retrievers and three chickens, so I've had plenty of time to reflect on the last sixty years of my life. I've found that probably the most important event in getting older and wiser is that by now I am more comfortable and confident in my skin and don't really care what other people think of me, what they think of my views, or what they think of what I am doing. I can stop trying to control things and the outcome and adopt a "whatever will be, will be" outlook. It's actually quite freeing to have put in the time and earned the right to be who I am.

So what does it look like to transition from that middle-aged person to the slightly older one that is no longer dealing with a nine-to-five grind? Do you think you might do something different in your life, but possibly more fulfilling?

Here are a few ideas that you might want to consider in order to enrich your life with something new, exciting, and challenging.

Volunteer: For years I have been volunteering at the zoo. I particularly enjoy playing "Mother Goose" at the "Boo at the Zoo" Halloween party they host once a year. Kids and animals, a great combo.

Bridge (Maj Jong or any card game): A few years ago I started taking bridge lessons. I took to it like a duck to water, and now I am teaching a beginning bridge class at the local community college.

Craigslist: I have found many interesting and creative opportunities checking out the part-time jobs on Craigslist, from working at a therapeutic riding academy to exercising horses.

Cooking: I love to cook and make a few special dishes. I worked on creating a specialty nut business to sell to brides and a few local artisan businesses around town. I obtained a cottage license that allowed me to make them in my home.

Hosting: For a year I have hosted a foreign exchange student. Though the pay is only a stipend, I have met some wonderful women from many different countries.

Renting: Let your house work for you. If you have some extra space like a bedroom or garage, rent it out. I drive a Mini Cooper, which doesn't take up much room, so I've rented out the other half of my garage to a vintage Corvette. I've also rented my home office to another therapist.

Dogs: I love dogs and have a half-acre all enclosed and fenced in, so I started a doggie day/overnight care service. I have two Golden Retrievers, so they get to have fun too while mom makes some extra cash and cuddles with other furry friends. If you don't have the space for a lot of roughhousing, then consider fostering a pet from a local animal shelter.

Hobbies: I'm a big believer in turning hobbies or passions into something that fills your days and might even turn a buck.

Education: I encourage everyone to learn something new, whether from the Internet or in a classroom. You can possibly make some new friends or learn a new trade.

Phew! . . . a lot of choices and opportunities to explore. For me, all of these activities keep me happy, healthy, and young at heart.

As I continue to grow into my new sixty-year-old skin, I enjoy exploring other ways to help myself grow and experience the richness of life even more. I have found that along with my personal daily check-in, mental images can help me as well.

Each and every day, we all wake up to the same problems or issues we went to sleep with. Often a good night's rest can present us with a new perspective, a fresh outlook on how we might wish to proceed with those concerns from the night before. Frequently, they don't seem to be as monumental as the day before, then we wonder what all the mental turmoil was about.

Slogans and mantras

Many of us have slogans or mantras that we play over and over again to quash our busy brains. Here are a few that I use and you might want to try if the ones you are using are a bit tired and need a vacation.

A little light gets you through the miner's tunnel

Life is more often a challenge than not. It can be as small as scheduling too many things in one day to concerns about your loved one's sobriety. Personally, I am not as carefree as I would like to be about what tomorrow will bring, so I find myself gripped with a bit of fear about the lack of control I have over my life. This visual has been very instrumental when I get the heebie-jeebies: I am walking in a dark tunnel with a miner's cap on that has that little flashlight attached to it. The light illuminates just enough space in front of me to keep me safe on my path. The ground is firm, and I know I am secure and protected even though I can't see much beyond the radiance of the small beam.

Like life, this semi-dark, semi-light passageway can go on for weeks, months, or maybe years. However, sometimes there is a fissure and the brightness from above floods in. These are the times in our lives when everything is in sync, everything is in unison, and comfort and joy abound. Usually, these are sporadic, but the experience fills our sails, so we are better able to handle the dark yet still lit tunnel of life that lies ahead.

Trusting that we are safe and on the right path, whether it is a small light that guides us or a blinding beam, builds character and fortitude and allows us to continue on with life's journey.

Brick by brick

The building of a business, a hobby, or any dream requires a tremendous amount of stick-to-it-tiveness. We have all heard that a journey begins with the first step; the visual I have adopted is brick by brick. I like the image of me building my own very personal structure literally one brick at a time, stepping back to take a gander every now and then, and knowing that I'm making progress even if it's at a snail's pace.

Listen for your direction

In the still of the morning as I am starting to gather my thoughts for the day, I take a moment or two and sit or lie quietly, open my heart and head, and listen for a bit of psychic instruction.

Often an unanswered issue will be presented to you if you can just listen for it. Don't ignore those voices that tickle your brain in presenting fresh options to explore regarding current personal and professional situations. You may just start implementing some of these mystical garbles that in time will prove to be very beneficial.

Quiet that screaming little kid in your head

When I am mentally ramped up and feel that a mini-meltdown

may be imminent, I picture this little kid bouncing off the walls of my brain like an old pinball machine. I hear myself telling her to calm down and come sit next to me. With flailing legs and arms, she slowly starts to settle in. I pet her leg gently, telling her it's all going to be okay, and eventually we both take a quiet, deep breath.

I know that I will be taken care of

This is my favorite. Knowing that if I do the next right thing that's in front of me, doing the footwork and letting the game come to me, then I will be taken care of. I might not see it at that moment or at the end of the day, but deep down I know that my needs will be met and probably better than I could ever imagine.

This visual finds you doing whatever makes you the happiest: a walk on the beach, sitting in a coffee shop, or hanging out with a four-legged friend.

These are just a few of my mental images that run like movie shorts in my brain. They are consistent and have become good, dependable friends. I can project whichever I need at any given time and feel better as quickly as a few seconds later.

Find the ones that work for you and keep them as your own private mental gold mines, artillery against whatever formidable foes you might be facing physically or emotionally.

Adding to our list of a healthier tomorrow is the concept of acceptance and deciding whether we want to accept the other person or not. This neutral attitude is actually my favorite mindset, for I have adopted an almost "I don't care" attitude. It's not meant to be callous, just freeing.

Lately, I have found some new clarity and freedom in accepting the other person for who and what they are and honestly concluding that I don't care what they do or say. When we accept the person for what they are, we might not like what they are doing, not approve of them, and therefore hold resentments.

For example, I'm of the opinion that one of my daughters is basically lazy. And though I know she loves me, she takes little or no interest in my life. I also hold the opinion that my other daughter is very rigid and doesn't roll with the punches very easily. She would rather opt out of an activity than do something that she doesn't want to do. Both of these girls are my daughters, and though I'm disappointed about some of their behaviors, I accept my daughters and find other areas that we can be compatible.

In some cases, acceptance has been known to breed resentment. It is how we handle that resentment that can possibly get us into trouble. Resentment can grow like a virus inside of us if left unchecked. I have found it helpful to hit my pause button when I feel that resentment growing and feel it may suddenly explode from being contained for too many years or through too many trials and tribulations.

You can't unring a bell. When our mouths act faster than our minds, the result may be a deep wound to the relationship—sometimes repairable, sometimes not. When we are faced with a person's personality foibles that we are not comfortable with, we need tools to consider how to handle them.

5 mental checkpoints:

1. Is this in the person's character, or are they having a bad day?

2. Would saying something fall on deaf ears and then a stronger resentment prevail between the two of you?

3. What is the source? Is this person struggling with jealousy or being pompous and arrogant to cover up some insecurity?

4. What can you be grateful for? Maybe you can be grateful you don't have to deal with this person on a daily basis. If your visits are infrequent, then you can have a specific plan as to how much time you can spend without feeling anxiety.

5. Are you prepared for the action that causes your resentment to continue? I know we all want to hope that tomorrow will be different, but if our expectations are at ground zero, then we can just say, "Oh, well," in our mind and move on.

The "I don't care" state of mind is much different than acceptance.

It is truly a place where one is comfortable with whatever actions or dialogue present themselves or not. The "I don't care" is not meant to be punishing, cruel, or "I'll show you," but truly a place of neutrality that permeates our thinking.

An example of this is that recently I have been spending time with a loved one who has been in and out of recovery. As he says, he has been in recovery for seventeen years though it hasn't been consistent. Our times together have been easy and comfortable. I am not holding my breath waiting for the proverbial other shoe of relapse to fall. I don't care whether he is clean or sober. It's his business, not mine.

Someone asked me the other day what I would do if he relapsed again. My answer was not full of dread or fear but was calm and neutral. I would implement my boundaries of spending time with a clean and sober person of six months. I'd start the clock ticking again, leaving the candle in the window burning in the hopes of yet another recovery process.

The best thing about the "I don't care" mental state is that there are no resentments or attempts to mold the other person into what we want them to be or do. It's not meant to be dismissive or mean; it's just a very calm effect that comes over us and therefore takes the pressure off of some relationships.

There is a difference between "I don't care" and "Who cares what happens or what they do?" Usually, the "who cares" attitude comes out of our resentment toward that person or that person's actions. It is viewed as a flippant, angry posture that can make others around us uncomfortable or think we are not being supportive.

It's a fine line between the acceptance of "I don't care" and the resentment of "Who cares?" Think about some of the people in your life and what category they fall into. Accept without resentment. Don't care because it's not in your power to change what that person or even the outside world does, and leave the sharp edges of the "Who cares?" mindset in a shoe box deep in a closet.

I promise that if you can honestly say with a smile on your face and a calm inner demeanor, "I don't care; it's not about me, but about them," then you will feel less burdened with old, smelly garbage.

Bottom line: Take care of yourself. You are important and your life, feelings, and emotions are super important too. This is not a dress rehearsal, and life goes by so very fast even if you feel that you are

constantly backstroking in the toilet. Climb out of that toilet, dry off, and head out the door for a new adventure, new friends, and new start in rebuilding your life. Your life is worth seeking a healthier tomorrow. I promise it can be found if you just take that tiny step forward!

Processing Questionnaire

- What are you happy with in your life?

- What would you like to change?

- What do you say or do when you need to get yourself off the ledge?

- How can you expand your horizons?

- Can you find your own personal mantra to help you get through the day or difficult moments?

- Find your passion! Can you give it some time either to grow and see if it's something you want to continue in your life or dump it and move on to something else?

- What is the biggest challenge for you in moving on, getting going, and trying something new and different?

CHAPTER 13

What other advice can you offer to help a loved one dealing with an alcoholic/addict?

I recommend you always keep in mind a series of questions that will be of help to you when you're dealing with the alcoholic/addict . . . or just living your own life in general. Every day some or all of these questions enter my mind. Sometimes I have the answers right then and there, other times I have to mull the situation over. Then in maybe a few hours, or sometimes a few days later, the answer comes to me. Nevertheless, keeping these questions in mind will make processing some emotions easier.

Questions to keep in mind:

1. **How important is it?**
   You've been wronged by someone. How important is it to retaliate? Will there be permanent damage if you do? Remember, you can't unring a bell. Or as my dad used to say, "Don't tell someone to go to hell as you might have to go down and get them."

   Hitting that pause button will help you get clarity on your next move. If you do want to call someone on their actions, be prepared that the relationship may either dissipate or get stronger. Resentment or appreciation will soon present itself, and you may find that it was a good thing you said something, or . . . "Darn, I wish I had kept my mouth shut."

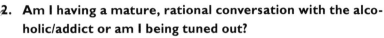

2. **Am I having a mature, rational conversation with the alcoholic/addict or am I being tuned out?**
   Remember that most times the alcoholic/addict wants to hear what they want to hear at that time or they are not interested in your opinion, reasoning, or thoughts. It's all about their wants and needs. If you don't fill the bill, then forget it. Stop wasting your breath. Leave the situation for the possibility of another time when *maybe* their thinking will not be under an influence that makes them unreachable.

3. **What's wrong with me? What's right with me?**
   This goes along with the all-important personal daily check-in. Morning and night I check in with myself to measure where my heart and head are. Am I uncomfortable with something that is minor that I can fix? Do I have to be patient to see how things unfold? Am I grateful or content with the things that are going right in my life at that moment?

4. **Are my boundaries secured for myself and with others?**
   Whether your boundaries are huge or small, it is important that you stay true to them. You took the time to instill them, so why not continue to enforce them? They should be as solid and habitual as brushing your teeth. Whether you find just two or twenty-two, stick to them and never budge.

5. **Am I moving my own life forward to experience new challenges and adventures?**
   Don't let dust settle around your ankles. Keep uncovering the next thing in store for you. Who knows, it may be the most important new plan in your life—life-changing as well as challenging. Check in with yourself and be honest as to whether you are moving ahead in a healthy way or making excuses like the alcoholic/addict. This is a no excuse, one-way street.
   Are your expectations reasonable for the day? Don't get ahead of yourself. Let things unfold as they should. Put one foot in front of the other, then let the game come to you. Trust that the outcome will be as it should.
   Are you being gentle and respectful to you? Whether it's a

spa treatment, drive through a forest, or walk on the beach . . .
take care of you! You are all you have, so be nice. And, make
sure others are nice to you as well, or *hasta la vista,* baby!

6. **Am I giving my pet extra kisses for their unconditional love,
   respect, and nonjudgmental attitude?**
   I left the best and easiest to the end. Can't be too tough to get
   a slobbery kiss, swinging tail, deep purring, or chirping to put
   a smile on your face. My two Golden Retrievers and my three
   chickens bring me joy, peace, love, respect, and . . . fresh eggs!!

A last final thought

I have found that it's easier to get the day going if I have a regular
dialogue with myself. It's not long or earthshaking. It's just good for
me and maybe it might work for you. When I'm taking my dogs for
their morning trail walk, I say to myself, "I have no idea what the day
will bring. But I will do the footwork and then let the game come to
me." I know I won't be disappointed as life is really oh so good!

Processing Questionnaire

- What are some important concepts that you can consider in your daily routine?

- How do you use them?

- Are they calming and helpful?

- Every few months do you add a few more and delete ones that seem stale or old hat?

ALSO BY CAROLE BENNETT

Available at your local bookstore or visit:

www.seahillpress.com

Made in the USA
Middletown, DE
10 August 2017